A MENTOR'S TOOLKIT
FOR CAREER
CONVERSATIONS

A COMPREHENSIVE GUIDE TO LEADING
CONVERSATIONS ABOUT CAREER PLANNING

ANN ROLFE

ISBN 978-0-9803564-6-5

If you would like to purchase slides, training session plans or other learning materials related to this book, please contact the author.

ann@mentoring-works.com.au

❀ Created with Vellum

CONTENTS

PART I
CAREER IN CONTEXT

PART II
THE MENTORING CONVERSATION

PART III
CAREER CONVERSATIONS

PART IV
TOOLS AND GUIDES

1

INTRODUCTION AND OVERVIEW

As a mentor, you might have career conversations with someone who wants to:

- **Develop:** build their capabilities, find ways to be better at what they do, enjoy their work more and have a more satisfying career.
- **Move:** gain knowledge, skills and experience to advance, get a better or different job.
- **Change:** do something completely different for a living.

It's a big responsibility because the mentee must make important decisions that have consequences on their lives, not just their livelihoods. Your job as a mentor is to ensure that they make informed decisions that are right for them.

I packed this book with resources to help you. It incorporates information and activities I have shared in workshops and webinars over my 30+ years experience in adult learning, career development and mentor training.

You can download printable versions of all the checklists and activities here: https://dl.bookfunnel.com/anzljazhx3

You and your mentee can access *Tools For Mentoring* a self-paced career-planning course of nine short videos online (included with your purchase of this book) here: http://mentoring-works.com/tools-for-mentoring/

Use the Password AMTCC21

If you want further assistance to develop your mentoring skills you may wish to purchase my book *Mentoring Mindset Skills and Tools*. Details here: http://mentoring-works.com/mentoring-mindset-skills-and-tools/

Or, take a look at the *Mentor Master Classes* video and ebook package here: http://mentoring-works.com/mentor-master-class-self-learning-package/

TOOLS & GUIDES LIST

You may have your own preferred sources, or your organisation may have additional resources for self-assessment or psychometric instruments. Use them as well, or instead of, the ones I've provided.

Online Learning

Tools for Mentoring is a self-paced career-planning course is made up of nine short (10-15 minute) videos and worksheets that you or your mentee can access anytime here:

http://mentoring-works.com/tools-for-mentoring/
Use the Password AMTCC21

Guides

- Quick Tips
- A Mentoring Code
- Pre-Meeting Checklist
- Post-Meeting Checklist
- First Meeting Agenda
- Review Meeting Worksheet
- Mentoring Evaluation Questions

Activities

1. Focus for Mentoring
2. Your Career Path to Date
3. Career Motivation
4. Where Am I Now?
5. Heroes Hall of Fame
6. Three-Dimensional Analysis
7. Values Discovery
8. Meeting Values
9. Achievements
10. Strengths Discovery
11. Strengths 30 Day Challenge
12. Write a Personal Mission Statement
13. Skills Audit
14. Functional Skills Checklist
15. Personal Attributes Checklist
16. Turn Personal Attributes into Skills
17. Transferrable Skills
18. Motivated Skills
19. Analyse Your Capabilities
20. Career Portfolio Checklist
21. Areas for Development
22. Deal With Your Inner Critic

You can download a printable PDF of all guides and activities to share with your mentee https://dl.bookfunnel.com/anzljazhx3

Other Suggested Activities

Online Strengths Assessment

The instrument I recommend for discovering talents and strengths and the one I use in coaching, mentoring programs and workshops is the CliftonStrengths Assessment. You can purchase this and do it online. It comes with detailed reports and a great deal of helpful information about using your results. Or, you can buy a hard copy book which comes with a code for the online instrument. www.gallupstrengthscentre.com

Knowdell Career Values Card Sort & Motivated Skills Card Sort

These offer an easy and enjoyable way to identify values and motivation. You can purchase packs of cards can which come with instructions, or use the card sorts online.

https://www.careerplanner.com/All-Knowdell-Products.cfm

MENTORING FOR CAREER OVERVIEW

The steps outlined here are simply a guide. You and your mentee could follow the sequence of aims and activities suggested, or choose a different pattern. The key is to be guided by and respond to the mentee's needs.

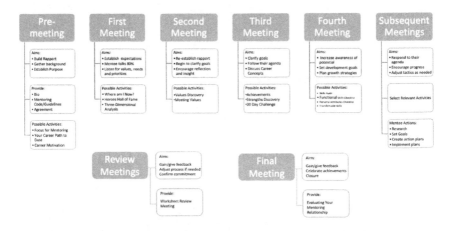

Figure 1: Meeting Aims and Activities

PRE-MEETING

Before you get together, I recommend you each provide a brief biography, just a paragraph or two of career highlights, special interests outside of work as well as career-related matters. You'll want to look for things you have in common and use the mentee's bio to develop questions to ask to draw them out if they are quiet or reserved.

It will help you both if you have some ideas about the mentee's reasons for wanting to be mentored. The activity Focus for Mentoring is a simple tick-the-box exercise that can help them identify their focus and help you develop questions. Alternatively, you could ask them to outline what they're hoping for from mentoring.

You can provide a copy of the Mentoring Code and Agreement Template from the Activities section of this book. If you are in a mentoring program, organisers may provide you with specific guidelines. You should also give the mentee an agenda for the first meeting, use the template to develop one that works for you. You will jointly plan the agenda for the subsequent meeting towards the end of each meeting and they can update that with a short list of topics or questions in a confirmation message/email a few days before.

FIRST MEETING

A big part of mentoring is getting to know one another. Don't be in a rush, it takes time to establish a relationship. You want to put them at ease, so they can open up and be candid with you and that means building rapport and trust. You need a harmonious connection, and them to have faith in your integrity, so that they will have the confidence to speak about their aspirations and concerns.

It is vital that early in the mentoring relationship you discuss expectations. It may be difficult for mentees to articulate exactly what they want, and it's fine to let aims and goals unfold over time, but you must be crystal clear about what is reasonable to expect of each other. If you are in a well run mentoring program, there will be explicit guidance, if you're on your own then it's wise to be straightforward in telling the mentee that you are not there to get them a job, do their research for them or give them inside information. You also should agree terms of engagement - the level and nature of contact, frequency and duration of meetings and confidentiality.

Apart from building rapport and trust, and establishing expectations, the first meeting will give you a sense of their current situation. However, you will also want a bit of future focus so that mentees leave with a sense of moving towards their aspirations. A vision of the future is very motivating.

Aim to ask questions that get them talking. You want them to be talking 80% of the time, so use follow-up questions to draw them out. Listen to what they say and not say. Try to pick up on and explore their values, needs and priorities. Reflect, summarise, and paraphrase their responses to encourage them to clarify and to confirm your understanding.

Towards the end of this (and every meeting) discuss what you might cover in the next one, and draft an agenda together. Schedule future meetings and ask them to send you a confirmation message/email a few days before it and include any additional topics, issues or questions they would like to put on the agenda. Ensure that they have committed to some actions to complete before you meet again.

Useful Questions, Conversation Starters and Follow-up Prompts:

"What do you want to get out of our mentoring?"

"How will we know if the mentoring is successful? What would we measure in twelve months' time?"

"Tell me about where you're at with your career, right now"

"Do you have thoughts about what you'd like to be next for you?"

"What is it that attracts you to that?"

"What is most important to you about..."

Remember, your role, at this stage in particular, is to be supportive and to validate their feelings. Simply accept what they say as their view of the world. When the relationship is well established, you may offer another perspective, opinion, or an alternate view that may be useful for them to consider.

SECOND MEETING

You will need to re-establish and continue to build rapport every time you meet. Allow a few minutes for small talk, getting coffee or settling, before you agree the agenda and get underway. If there is a lot on the agenda, have them set some priorities to cover this time, with others to be deferred. Review any activities they completed or actions they have taken since you last met. Again, support them to be the one doing most of the talking, encouraging them with non-verbal and minimal responses (nodding, "mm hm etc.). Prompt their reflection to draw out insight. Sometimes you'll need to watch the expressive language of their face and allow them time to process their thoughts by staying silent. In this meeting, you may begin to firm up the aims of your mentoring and the goals the mentee would like to achieve.

Useful Questions, Conversation Starters and Follow-up Prompts:

"So, what's been happening since we last met?"

"Which of these (agenda) items is most important for us to cover today?"

"What stood out for you from this exercise?"

"What comes to mind when you reflect on that?"

"Tell me more about..."

THIRD MEETING

Their goals should be clearer by now, but they may still evolve and change over time. Continue to follow their agenda and respond to their needs. If it is appropriate to do so, introduce some concepts described in Part 1 of this book, such as the changing career landscape, or career phases or life balance. You will have more input in this type of conversation, but approach it as collaboration and discovery rather than instruction.

Useful Questions, Conversation Starters and Follow-up Prompts:

"What does (the activity) tell you about what you want from your career?"

"What does this information (research they've done or an activity) mean for you?"

"How might this impact on your career decisions?"

"How can we use this to frame your goals?"

"What is your top priority, right now/for the next three months/this year?"

Fourth Meeting

By now, the conversation may have moved into the "how might you get there" phase. The activities they've completed will highlight talents and strengths as well as values, preferences and priorities. They may have strengths that are under-utilised or underdeveloped, so they may need to plan their development, or they could be ready to research possibilities and choose their career direction. A conversation that invites them to compare and contrast their current situation and what they want in future will help them identify where they need to take action. Help them set realistic goals and plan practical strategies. Bigger, long-term goals will need to be broken down into manageable steps.

Useful Questions, Conversation Starters and Follow-up Prompts:

"Tell me about your vision of the future you'd like"

"When you think about where you are now and where you'd like to be in the future, what do you see as the major differences?"

"What would need to change for this to happen?"

"What skills and abilities would help you get there?"

"What else would you need to develop?"

"How might you gain the knowledge and skills you need?"

Subsequent Meetings

As mentoring progresses, it becomes more unique. Goals, needs and directions will unfold. You can still be the wise guide by using the process illustrated in the Framework for the Mentoring Conversation, but is is a framework to support you, not a rigid set of rules, so you'll need to be flexible. Respond to their agenda and make sure they are making informed decisions by suggesting they research reliable and up-to-date sources, consider options and move forward. As they try new things, not all will go to plan. There could be unintended or unexpected outcomes. These could be beneficial or not, so you will help them find ways adjust to their new circumstance or change tactics as they go.

REVIEW MEETINGS

After three or four meetings, schedule a meeting to review your mentoring process. Give them a heads-up about what you'll cover in this conversation and that you want their honest appraisal so that you can improve both the effectiveness and the enjoyment of mentoring together. Seek and be open to feedback from the mentee and be willing to adapt or negotiate ways to proceed. The first review meeting should include the choice to opt out if it's not working for either of you and you can't rectify the problems. If you are in a mentoring program, the coordinator should be able to help get the relationship back on track or dissolving it.

The following questions are on a worksheet that you should provide to the mentee so that they can prepare for your first review meeting. A scaled down review meeting, perhaps using just questions 2, 3, and 6 should suffice at intervals afterwards and may not need a separate meeting.

What have we achieved, so far, as a result of mentoring?

What works well in our mentoring?

What's not working so well?

What are you enjoying/not enjoying in the mentoring?

What, done differently, could improve our mentoring?

What could each of us do differently or better?

Overall, how do you feel about our mentoring?

Do you want to continue?

FINAL MEETING

In a mentoring program, there is usually a set endpoint and may be some sort of event to provide closure and celebrate achievements. If not, provide Evaluating Your Mentoring Relationship to the mentee and use these discussion starters to share feedback:

What did you each get out of the mentoring experience?

To what degree was good rapport established?

Were the mentee's needs addressed?

Did you achieve the goals nominated at the outset of the mentoring?

Were meetings the right duration and frequency?

Has the mentee's ability to produce and sustain self-development improved because of mentoring?

How satisfied is the mentee with counsel and advice provided?

Was constructive and encouraging feedback provided when needed?

Was the mentee encouraged to accept responsibility for his or her own development?

What demonstrable outcomes can we attribute to the mentoring relationship?

How do you each feel about the mentoring?

PART I

CAREER IN CONTEXT

These three chapters provide useful background information and key issues to keep in mind when discussing career decisions with mentees.

The Changing Career Scene looks at the dynamic world of work, including the impact of the COVID-19 pandemic on the work environment.

Career Phases outlines different concerns people may have at different ages and stages of their career

Work/Life Balance offers practical suggestions for addressing one of the central problems of workers today.

1

THE CHANGING CAREER SCENE

Mentors are often sought by people wanting career advice. They may ask you because you are a role model, you have experience, have advanced your career, or in a position they aspire to. You have valuable information to share and they may come to you with questions about how to move into a new role, how to move up, or into a leadership role, how to reinvigorate their career, re-enter or remain in the workforce or how to achieve work/life balance.

People perceive a mentor as a wise guide and, if you are prepared to be a mentor, you need to do more than answer specific questions. You need to lead a process that enables the mentee to discover options and make informed choices about their future. Before you can give advice that will be of value, you need to understand what they really need and want and what their personal priorities are.

Going deeper into their questions using the activities in this book, you'll help them clarify what they're really looking for from their career, how it fits with the way they want to live life, and what they can realistically aspire to.

Equally important is understanding career fundamentals. Knowing and sharing essential facts about careers will increase the effectiveness of the mentoring. You'll give better advice; they'll make better decisions, and both the process and the outcomes will be more satisfying to each of you.

Changing Career Scenarios

The world of work constantly changes as jobs become extinct and new ones emerge. Even the term "job" is outdated now, positions are more often described as roles. Roles are constantly evolving. People seldom stay in one occupation all their working lives, let alone with one employer or one job, as once might have been the norm. Whereas once it was safe to invest in education or training for a particular occupation, now a degree or qualification in any field does not always lead to work in that area and is no guarantee of employment. An occupation in high demand today may be redundant by the time a qualification has been obtained. Be aware that what was once true, or true for you, may no longer the case in today's job market . Look at some examples below.

Old	New
Stay in a job at least 2 years. Job hopping looks bad on your resume	The average job tenure (all age groups) is 3 years 4 months. Younger people are more mobile. Show that the learning and experience gained adds value.
Gaps in your resume will do against you	Travel, caring for a family member, volunteering and retraining are valuable. Frame gaps as learning experiences skill building
Don't tell your boss you're looking for another job	There's less risk these days. Most places want employees to leave on good terms. So, unless you have reason to think they'll make it tough, tell your boss. They may make a counter-offer or help you find new opportunities within the organization.
Once you leave you can never go back	Organisations see the value in their employees gaining experience elsewhere and may welcome back a valuable employee
Always be on the look out for a better job	Always look for ways to learn and grow, take satisfaction in your work, and enjoy what you do
Career success means upward progression, more money and a management role	Success means different things to different people and what's important changes at their life stages. Work/life balance and non-managerial specialist or technical roles often provide more satisfaction

Figure 2: Old, once accurate observations about careers and new views

It is likely that, every employee will need to "re-tool" to meet the changing requirements of the workplace. Some will need to do so several times. This might mean short, intensive study to repurpose existing skills and giving them micro-credentials[1] to transition to new jobs or a complete reinvention.

The obvious and biggest issue shaping the future of work is technology. Artificial Intelligence (AI), automation and robotics are taking over repetitive and technical jobs, making many redundant. And, lest you think this is only affecting low-skilled and blue-collar workers, Here are some statistics from the Gallup research back in 2015: 70% of young Australians are going into jobs that will be automated within 10-15 Years. 28% of employers say students are not prepared for the workplace. 50% of young Australians are being educated for dying jobs. Some of the disappearing jobs may surprise you. They include doctors, lawyers and public servants. University of Sydney professor of data science and machine learning Hugh Durrant-Whyte says "All jobs that are primarily analysis are capable of automation." [2] It's not all bad news though, because of course there will be new jobs, just not as we know them.

What change means is that the skills in demand change, and transferrable skills — those you can use in many settings — are going to be more important. Helping your mentee identify the full range of their skills will set them up for the future.

1. Growth Mindset
2. Continuous Learning
3. Critical Thinking
4. Survival Skills (overcoming challenges)
5. Resilience, Curiosity
6. Flexibility
7. Dedication
8. Coaching Mindset
9. Comfort With Ambiguity
10. Thriving in a Virtual Environment

Figure 3: Forbes Human Resource Council Expert Panel
The Top 10 Skills Recruiters Are Looking For In 2021.

Employment is increasingly globalised. The trend that began long prior to 2020 included outsourcing jobs to countries where labour is cheaper and less regulated. It sped up when the pandemic taught us that working from home was not only feasible but necessary.

How Mentors Can Help

You can't expect to be totally across the ever-changing career scene. However, you can familiarise yourself with career trends by reading publications like Forbes Magazine, Harvard Business Review (you can access a limited number of articles free online) and the careers section of local newspapers or business magazines. While each person is unique, books like Daniel Pink's *Drive* provide very useful, research-based insight into what really motivates people (spoiler alert, its autonomy, mastery and purpose). I've listed other recommended reading in the References and Resources section of this book.

Is it even possible to give worthwhile advice in an ever-changing environment? Yes! It's just not as straight-forward as telling people what to do. Rather, it's about helping them explore options, make informed decisions and take the actions most likely to get the outcomes they want.

Don't do all the work yourself! Ask the mentee to research reliable, authoritative sources. They can gather the details then discuss options. Help them critique the information they gather and use it in practical ways. Help them discern what's meaningful and relevant to them. Keep in mind, your aim is to support them to make informed decisions for themselves.

Figure 4: A Mentor can offer the mentee

CAREER CONSTRAINTS

Every mentee will have real and perceived constraints or barriers to deal with. You can help a mentee set goals and plan strategies to overcome obstacles. Others will be outside their control yet can be addressed to some extent, and some will require specialist input. Often the circumstances can be changed over time, so long-term career aims must be complemented with shorter-term strategies to gain work/life satisfaction. Be aware that career issues are complex and may need in-depth exploration. You may want to park them until goals are firmed up and you're into action planning. I intend the table below as a quick overview of common constraints, considerations and basic strategies only.

Common Constraints	Considerations	Basic Strategies
Job market constraints	Is it a perception or fact? Are they able to re-locate for opportunities? Are goals defined too narrowly?	Have them research the job market Self-assess to identify alternative occupations Expand possibilities
Lack of education, training, qualification or credentials	What are the real requirements for work in their preferred field? Is upskilling feasible?	Investigate on-the-job learning options If qualifications are required, invest in education if possible
Ageism, sexism, racism	Is a structural problem within the organization? Is it a personal bias of an individual blocking them?	Seek organisations with stated diversity policies and demonstrated inclusion practices Look for more supportive environments
Low self-confidence	Is it really confidence issues or structural barriers that constrain them?	Explore the evidence Help them review and identify achievements and strengths Learn public speaking
Non-negotiable commitments eg. Co-parenting/co-careers Elder care	Is the situation permanent or temporary? Have shared responsibilities at home been negotiated fairly?	Set long-term goals but look for ways to increase work/life satisfaction Specialist counselling may be called for
Financial eg. mortgage, credit card debt, personal loans, student loans	Is it income or spending that is the problem?	Requires specialist input eg. budgeting, mortgage shopping for lower interest rates
Poor social skills	Is it just their natural temperament misunderstood? In what ways do social skills hold them back?	Involvement in activities with others with shared interests Specialist coaching or training

Figure 5: Overview of Common Constraints, Considerations and Basic Strategies

AGE-RELATED Pressure Points

We used to talk about "mid-life crisis", but it has become clear that there are various ages and stages in life where people take stock and reconsider the track they're on with life and career. It doesn't have to be a crisis, but it may be time for a change. For some people, it's their early thirties when they may "hear the biological clock ticking", see friends marrying and starting families, or simply question if where they are in their career is all that it could be. Parents returning to work after a break to care for their children may struggle with unreasonable expectations and lack of support. They may take part-time or job-share roles for reduced work hours. This can be a useful strategy or a career setback, as they are often overlooked for promotions. Managers may hold false assumptions about their capability and commitment against them. Some people will start their own businesses for a more family-friendly solution. Mid-forties to fifties can provide a challenge as people think about what they've achieved, whether it's all they hoped for, when they'll get some "me time" and if it's too late to start over. This is frequently when ageism kicks in when applying for roles. Often, incorrect assumptions about how long they have to give the organisation, their ability to learn, and their mastery of technology work against them. Past sixty, some employees have concerns about being passed over for new challenges. On the other hand, they may look forward to a whole new chapter when they can do what they really want. Their maturity and experience may be undervalued. Older people may worry about retirement finances. Many women will live in poverty once they can no longer work. Others with the benefit of superannuation or financial assets will be quite well prepared. Many people in their mid-sixties put retirement off as the pandemic affected their savings in 2020. The Australian Government has raised the age at which people can apply for a pension. Some people don't want to retire and expect to keep working into their eighties.

The Work from Home (WFH) Revolution

Since the pandemic, work is no longer 9-5 office centric. Working from home — at least some of the week — has become widely accepted, and while this may assist with work/life balance, the opposite may also be true. People may feel like there's no "off switch" and this impacts on work/life balance, relationships and stress. Reduced work/life boundaries can reduce mental wellbeing. Many work-from-home set-ups are less than ideal, digital communication and technical problems are challenges and yet, productivity remains high (85% of Australian Knowledge workers say they are as productive or more productive).

Working from home will affect on careers. Workers are more isolated and have less opportunity for informal mentoring and networking. Working from home reduces employees' exposure and perhaps chances to develop their profile and attract attention with their skills and abilities. There are no chats in lunch room or wash room, by the water cooler or out with the smokers on breaks. They may miss out on information about roles they could apply for or projects they could join.

Starting even casual and informal mentoring allows people to develop rapport, reach out and find common ground. Making contact and strengthening connections with others will overcome the isolation felt by working from home or in an environment where you must maintain physical distance. As a mentor you can help them overcome the obstacles to career development that working from home may bring. Your conversations will keep them focussed and proactive in managing their career and perhaps track down opportunities they may otherwise miss.

Career Mobility

Some people are more driven than others to seek promotion. For them, career advancement means moving up. However, with flatter organisations, better educated employees and competition there are fewer opportunities for promotion. Not everyone wanting to move up is suited to it, so it's important they get a realistic view of the requirements and their capabilities. Some people seek the status and money that may come with promotion, but have not thought through the downside of the job, if it is a management role it could take them away from aspects of their work they love, burden them with administrative tasks and force them to manage people. For these reasons, we need to help mentees expand their horizons about advancing their career. People have more mobility (agility or resilience if you want the buzz words) when they are continually developing their knowledge, skills and experience.

Career conversations that explore what they are really looking for from their work will allow them to select the moves most likely to satisfy them.

2

CAREER PHASES

Today's school leaver is likely to have 17 different employers and move through at least 5 distinct career changes instead of the job-for-life scenario cherished by older generations. Finding satisfying and meaningful work means exploring options and lifelong learning.

Age Group	Average Job Tenure
Under 25	1 year 8 months
25-35	2 years 8 months
35-44	4 years
45+	6 years 8 months
Average	3 years 4 months

Figure 6: Job tenure by age group in Australia Source
HILDA, Department of Employment

EARLY CAREER

Students in the last years of high school can be overwhelmed by strenuous study demand and exams and concerns about their future. They often believe success or failure depends on their performance in their final exams. They may have unrealistic expectations of themselves and/or burdened by a desire to please their parents. There may be an all-or-nothing theme in their thinking. All of this creates a huge amount of stress.

Your aim as a mentor of anyone at this stage is to reassure and support them while they explore their options. While you want them to do as well as they can in exams, it isn't the end of the world if their scores aren't what they hoped for. These numbers are only meaningful in terms of entry to particular university courses. Students may be best to access specialist services regarding career options, study choices and stress management, so help them find the appropriate resources.

Where you can offer most assistance is helping them make informed decisions about choosing to continue their education at a college, university or trade or technical courses, or to seek an entry-level job. They may also need to discuss the pros and cons of narrowing their aims to a particular trade or profession versus a broader, more general, further education. Of course, the financial implications of their choice will be a factor in decision-making. Your conversations should draw out their interests, aptitudes, talents, and strengths. It's a good idea to demonstrate that no career decision is irrevocable and they will have options as their their journey unfolds, many of which neither of you can know now.

Prior to 2020, better off students often took a "gap year" to do casual work, save and travel. This was a pressure relief, a pause from study, a chance to meet new people, and an opportunity to develop independence, maturity and perspective useful for making career decisions. The impact of COVID-19 on health, finances and travel is likely to restrict this practice, but it is still an option to regard the twelve months after they finish school as a way to explore, get experience and gather information about what suits them and what doesn't.

For those who take degree courses, it's worth investigating graduate programs offered by private and public sector organisations. Most will have representatives at careers fairs on campus and they often look to hire promising students before they graduate.

Potential employers sometimes offer young people unpaid internships. These may be good to gain work experience, however sometimes they exploit young workers, so your mentee will need to weigh up the cost/benefits of such arrangements.

Career Change at Any Age

Sometimes people will proactively seek change for their own reasons, but circumstances sometimes thrust change upon them. Here in Australia, we've recently seen the death of car manufacturing throw many people out of work. The energy industry is transitioning which will mean coal miners will lose jobs. COVID-19 decimated the arts, hospitality and tourism. Economic, technological, social and political changes will impact on most industries and occupations. Such disruptions do not just end jobs; new ones emerge and evolve, but it may not be as simple as stepping from one role to another.

For those who have not sought change, particularly with forced redundancy or retrenchment, there may be a period of grieving and learning to let go of the old before they can contemplate their future. Many people have their sense of self-identity tied to their occupation, so losing their job is like losing part of themselves.

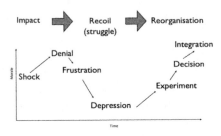

Figure 7: Kubler-Ross Change Model

The Kubler-Ross Change Model (previous page) shows the roller coaster of emotions a person who has lost their job may fee. As you can see, they may need specialist counselling rather than mentoring at first. I wrote an ebook *Mentoring in the Current Crisis* early in 2020. You can download it here: https://dl.bookfunnel.com/jkonfhqdjo

Career Plateau

A career plateau is when a person reaches the top of their game and feels there's nothing left to learn. Or, when there is a lack of opportunities to take on additional responsibilities, or if employers overlook them for advancement. For some this is a satisfying period of coasting, easing the pressure of learning and development, resting on the laurels of previous achievement. Such a strategy can be dangerous in the fast-paced work-world of today where yesterday's knowledge, skills and accomplishments are quickly superseded and may become redundant. For others, a career plateau is frustrating. They find the lack of growth opportunities stymieing and lose enthusiasm for the job.

This is often a time for workers to re-evaluate their career path. Frequently this coincides with a re-examination of life — taking a fresh look at goals, values, needs, interests and preferences. Help them consider choices and change. This can lead to a whole new blossoming of people's talents that I call this career renaissance.

. . .

LATE CAREER

With longer lifespans, people may want to reignite their career path or move with joy into an encore career that they've been waiting all their life to try. Some will explore new options and happily begin again in a new occupation. They'll pursue new goals, or ones for which previous demands left little time. Some people keep satisfaction throughout their career and have no desire to change or retire. Others count the days until they can stop work, but many dread the time when they can no longer work because it will mean living in poverty, or because they fear life will have no meaning without paid work. As a mentor, you can help them explore options and choose what is right for them.

While the challenges people face are different at different ages and stages, your role as a mentor is the same: You'll help them take stock of where they are now, make informed choices about where they want to be, formulate plans about how they might get there and take actions with your support and encouragement.

3

WORK/LIFE BALANCE

I called this chapter work/life balance because that's the term that most people use, but I have a problem with the wording for a three reasons. One is that the language may set up a mindset that pits work and life against one another. The second is the implication that balance means work and life are of equal importance and may have equal time and energy devoted to them. This suggests work is half of all there is. I guess the third point is, can you really carve out and separate work from life?

I'd rather think of life balance, which to me means living in ways that satisfy your human needs and create wellbeing. Wellbeing is not just a "warm fuzzy" nice to have element of work-life. Wellbeing has serious health implications for work, health and society, as shown below.

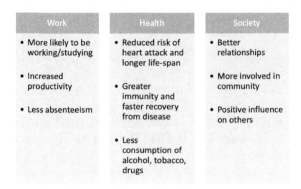

Work	Health	Society
• More likely to be working/studying	• Reduced risk of heart attack and longer life-span	• Better relationships
• Increased productivity	• Greater immunity and faster recovery from disease	• More involved in community
• Less absenteeism		• Positive influence on others
	• Less consumption of alcohol, tobacco, drugs	

Figure 8: Impact of Wellbeing

There are four key elements that contribute to life balance and well-being, as shown below. If we accept these four elements needed to ensure balance and wellbeing, it puts work into a larger context. Work can satisfy some, but not all, our needs. Recognising the areas in which work fulfils us, or not, can enable us to seek new or different solutions to career issues, or find what we need in other areas of life.

Figure 9: Four Elements of Life Balance

PHYSICAL

Few of us can provide for our own physical needs without money. We need food, clean water and shelter to stay alive, and many other tangible things that make life enjoyable. So, most of us have to work to earn the money that pays for living and lifestyle. If we can't provide for ourself financially, it may force us to depend on partners, family or the state to provide for us. This has implications for our physical, emotional, mental, and spiritual wellbeing.

Work that robs us of the ability to look after our physical health - if we don't get enough exercise or relaxation, if we sit all day, or work in dirty, unhealthy or dangerous conditions, it undermines our physical wellbeing. Long hours and shift work are detrimental to health. So balance means that we need to counteract any negative impact of our work.

Emotional

Emotional wellbeing is being happy, although it's more than that. Happiness is the sum total of experiencing positive emotions such as joy, compassion, and satisfaction with life.

It is hard to separate emotional wellbeing from social wellbeing. Way back, Maslow identified a sense of belonging as the next level of human needs after basic needs for food, water, shelter and safety. We all need the social interaction that friends, family, society, and for many, the workplace provides. Emotionally, work can give us a sense of purpose, meaning and identity; socially it gives us connection, a tribe, interaction and belonging.

Bullying, harassment and discrimination — sexism, racism, agism — loneliness and isolation, or a hostile environment, destroy people's emotional wellbeing at work. These factors impact on emotional, mental and physical wellbeing. If they are structural issues they are difficult for an individual to overcome. If your mentee is dealing with these they may need specialist support.

MENTAL

Most people want life to be mentally stimulating, with enough challenge to keep them interested, but not so much that they feel overwhelmed (think Goldilocks - not too big, not too small, but just right). People need a sense that they are capable and competent. Most enjoy the opportunity to grow and learn continually. This is what we hope for from work.

Mental wellbeing is as important as physical health and is closely linked to both physical and emotional wellbeing. We need to ensure that work does not negatively affect mental wellbeing.

SPIRITUAL

There is a human need for meaning and purpose in life that is satisfied by spirituality of some description. It may or may not include religious belief. Spiritual wellbeing is about the inner self connecting with others, art, music, literature, nature, or a higher power. Spirituality involves making a contribution to the world. Some people can express this through their work, perhaps being involved with an organisation that does good works for humanity, the environment, the arts or science. An increasing number of organisations are including corporate giving, social responsibility and philanthropy in their missions.

Your mentee will need to address their need for spiritual wellbeing in the way they live their life, and perhaps within their work. They may not speak about spirituality, but there needs to be a space in life for love, and time to appreciate and enjoy art, music, literature, nature, spiritual beliefs or whatever nurtures their spirit.

So, if work/life balance is a topic your mentee wants to explore, you'll need to prepare for conversations about these four areas of life. Because each of us is unique, your mentee's needs will differ from your own. Your aim will be to listen well and prompt their introspection. They will need time to reflect and delve into their needs. There are several activities in this book that will assist the process.

Factors Contributing to Burnout

- Workload
- Time pressures
- Manager pressure
- Personal pressure
- Job insecurity

Figure 10: Factors Contributing to Burnout

Many people feel overwhelmed with competing demands as they struggle and juggle work hours and non-work commitments, relationships, home, health and leisure. Often they have precious little little time for themselves. Whether it's families with young kids to drop off and pick up from care or school, parents rushing kids to sport, music or other activities nights and weekends, people in high pressure occupations working very long hours, those combining work and study, elder care responsibilities, or those who have to manage two or three insecure jobs to make ends meet, life balance is a challenge.

If this is the case for your mentee, you are going to have to help them sort out:

- Personal values and priorities
- Good time management practices
- Ways they can nurture their health and wellbeing in all four areas of life balance

Life balance issues result from people feeling conflicted. They feel pressured by what they should do and they may feel somewhat help-less to change their situation. So mentors need to help mentees see what they can change and what they can't.

The Circle Of Influence

In any situation, there are things you can control and things you can't. In the illustration below, the centre circle represents that which is within your power to influence. The outer circle represents aspects of the situation that may concern you, but over which you have little control.

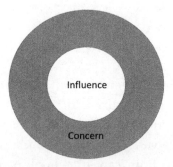

Figure 11: The Control Principle. Inspired by Covey, S. (1989)
The Seven Habits of Highly Effective People. The Business
Library

In any situation, what a person has most influence over, the epicentre of their circle of control, is themself. You have control over what you do, what you say and what you think.

Use this concept to help the mentee recognise what they can control and what they can't because this immediately reduces stress and allows them to focus their energy and efforts on where they will do most good. It enables them to choose actions that will produce posi-tive outcomes.

In a career conversation, a mentor enables the mentee to explore options and make informed decisions about the actions they will take. You want to empower them. The classic work by Stephen Covey[1] suggests that in any situation we may take one of two basic positions: reactive or proactive.

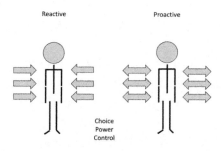

Figure12: Reactive/Proactive

When we take the reactive position, we see external events impacting upon us. We feel that we have little or no choice, power or control over what is happening.

Reactiveness is a common response to overwhelming or unexpected and unwelcome events. As a short-term, necessary, protective strategy, it allows us, at a subconscious level, to believe that we are not responsible for external events that impact upon us. We ease stress by blaming events, circumstances or other people for our current situation. The reactive position is a useful coping mechanism.

In the longer-term, however, the reactive strategy loses its effectiveness. If the focus remains on the lack of control over events, we may continue to cope, but frustration and bitterness exacerbate stress. Helplessness and hopelessness can lead to depression and an unwillingness, or inability, to move on. If we stay "stuck" in the reactive position, we remain a victim of circumstances.

When we take the proactive position, we see external events impact upon us, but we recognise that we have some choice, power and control over what happens *next*. Taking the proactive position allows us to *move beyond* merely coping with events and easing stress. Instead of being at the mercy of the influence of external events, we recognise that we can influence some aspects of the situation.

As a long-term strategy, the proactive position is effective and necessary. We live in a world of uncertainty, change, and stressful events. Proactivity is the key to managing this. Having choices, options, a range of alternatives from which to choose empowers us. The more we make sound choices and act on them, the more we take control of life. Realising that *what we do* influences the circumstances of our living refocuses our attention on changing the situation. However, we must take care to ensure that we do not take this to extremes. We are not responsible for everything that happens. If blaming others is counterproductive, constantly blaming ourselves is equally dysfunctional.

In career management, taking a proactive position means choosing a career direction, planning what you need to do and taking action. Often, people get stuck in the reactive position because they are not taught career management skills. They lack information on which to base their choices, or have no career planning support or resources. Your mentoring will enable the mentee to become more proactive in their career. It will not only assist them with career decisions today, it will help build resilience for the future and in other parts of their life.

PART II

THE MENTORING CONVERSATION

This part of the book offers the fundamental concepts and techniques of mentoring.

Mentoring: a Safe Space shows how to create a non-threatening environment that allows the mentee to speak candidly.

A Framework for the Conversation provides the simple and easy to remember four-step process to lead a mentoring conversation.

Develop Talents and Strengths outlines why strengths development is important, what strengths are, and how you lead people to realise their potential.

4

MENTORING: A SAFE SPACE

> ## A Mentoring Conversation is one where:
>
> *people are safe to explore thoughts and feelings.*
> *They use critical, creative and above all reflective thinking*
> *to gain insight and generate possible options.*
> *They make informed choices as they decide on goals and*
> *actions.*
> *They are assisted, as needed, to plan the way forward,*
> *and then they are supported and encouraged as they*
> *implement their plan.*

Figure 13: Definition of a Mentoring Conversation

For a mentoring conversation to take place, mentors need to create a safe space, an environment where people will open up, be able to speak, and feel heard without fear. A safe space is the foundation of a mentoring conversation. It means having a physical and emotional environment with no sense of threat. And creating space where there is trust and rapport between the mentor and mentee.

To create a safe space for a mentoring conversation, begin by considering the physical environment. Choose a neutral setting, like a meeting room rather than your office, unless you are meeting virtually. You need a place that offers enough quiet and privacy but is not too secluded. Your non-verbal communication should signal safety as well. Be aware of tone of voice and body language that can be perceived as threatening.

We need to understand just how easily a look, a word or gesture can trigger a threat response. We evolved from ancient ancestors whose survival depended on their ability to react fast to any threat. They did so by defending themselves, running away, or hiding. Today, your evolved brain is still constantly vigilant, scanning the environment five times per second for potential threats. In every interaction with other people your brain is asking: am I safe or is there a threat? This goes on at a subconscious level. If any kind of threat registers, an instantaneous reaction in the limbic area of the brain triggers the fight/flight/freeze reaction. Hormones flood the brain, causing us to hear differently, process differently, and behave differently. In a heightened state of alertness, people often become defensive. They are less likely to open up and risk vulnerability.

In a mentoring conversation the biggest fears are likely to be judgment, criticism, or ridicule, but the vigilant brain is sensitive to environmental stimuli. Things like large desk or chair are symbols of power and status. A closed door may cause concern to some. The limbic area of the brain can't tell the difference between a genuine threat and an imagined one. You know this if you've ever watched a scary movie and felt your heart thumping, or nearly jumped out of your seat when the on-screen raptor leaped at you. Not only that, but once the fight/flight/freeze reaction has been primed, you stay jumpy for some time! People are especially primed for a threat response when they experience chronic, low grade stress, are subject to discrimination, harassment, or are survivors of abuse. No matter how mature, or able to self-regulate we are, perceived threat effects our ability to communicate.

However, there is good news. As well as threat, the brain also responds to what neuroscientists call reward. As social animals, humans' greatest rewards come from our interactions with others. We *need* relationships and communication. Loneliness is harmful to our health, and solitary confinement is a high-level punishment.

Neuroscientists talk about social drivers that create either threat or reward. Understanding the social drivers can allow us to reduce threat reactions and enhance reward responses in others.

We can think of social drivers as levers. When the lever in the forward position, the brain perceives reward and safety and responds with trust. Push the lever the other way and the message is threat and it triggered defences.

Dr Norman Chorn and Dr. Terri Hunter of the Brainlink Group, use the acronym SAFETY to help us remember the five social drivers.

Security: certainty, predictability, stability

Autonomy: freedom to decide and choose

Fairness: equity, transparency, social justice

Esteem: status in relation to others, recognition

Trust: belonging to a group or tribe, feeling safe in relationships with others

Your personal priority within these: the one that's a hot button for you.

Figure 14: Five Social Drivers. Source Dr Norman Chorn and Dr. Terri Hunter of the Brainlink Group

Security

We use routines, habits, and the rules of thumb to make millions of minor decisions each day. These default settings allow us to do things without thinking, it's as if the brain is on autopilot. This frees up the executive function (neo cortex) to deal with immediate and important cognitive tasks.

The brain hates change, disruption and the unexpected, because switching off auto-pilot to use the executive function to process the new data and act deliberately, instead of out of habit, requires effort and uses vital energy.

Security to the brain means routine, ordinary, no surprises. So, you are likely to experience ambiguity, confusion, or unmet expectations as a threat, and your brain will prime you for defensiveness. Familiarity, previous or similar experience, clear expectations, being prepared, forewarned or briefed about expectations signal safety to your brain.

Autonomy

Adults want to be self-directing. Most of us hate rigid rules, being given orders or micromanaged. We resent top-down planning that robs us of input and feels disempowering to you and threatening to the brain. When we feel we are in control, have independence and choices, or can work in collaboration, the brain perceives reward.

Fairness

What will push this lever into threat is unfair treatment, injustice, the perception of favouritism, preferential treatment, or arbitrary decisions. The brain perceives reward when there is transparency, logical rationale for decisions, and equity.

Esteem

We instinctively understand the importance of status. High-status individuals get more. Whether it's food, money, sex, the corner office, the car or parking spot, or better assignments at work.

The brain is constantly evaluating our status in relation to others. Feeling judged or looked down on, negative feedback, not winning in a competitive situation, lack of money or having to do the dirty work, can all lower self-esteem and raise defensiveness. Mastery — self-efficacy, seeing yourself as competent, being treated with respect, being acknowledged, positive feedback and praise are rewarding.

Trust

Rejection, isolation, loneliness, feeling different and socially disconnected are very threatening and cause great pain. The brain experiences social pain in the same way as physical pain. Trust means we feel safe. Inclusion, rapport, empathy and friendship are rewards that bring us closer toward each other.

Your Dominant Social Driver

All five social drivers are important, but usually one is more dominant than others in each of us. That means that it is easier to trigger brain response - trust or defend - in this area. Your dominant driver will filter your perception of others and events.

You are most likely to use your dominant driver when interacting with people, but if they have a different one, yours has less appeal, and it's harder to build the relationship. So, you'll need to cover all five unless you know their preferred driver and can "speak their language". Here's how:

In MENTORING, you build **security** by:

- Agreeing ground rules
- Discussing expectations
- Sharing an agenda prior to meeting

As A MENTOR, you preserve the mentees **autonomy** by:

- Listening more than you speak and asking more than telling
- Encouraging them to make their own decisions
- Discussing their intentions, actions and likely outcomes so that they can take responsibility

As A MENTOR you can show **fairness** through:

- An open mind that sees both sides of an argument
- Describe situations from different perspectives
- Champion equity

As A MENTOR, maintain the mentee's **esteem** through:

- Treat them as a colleague, an equal, and don't patronise them
- Be slow to give advice, even when asked — facilitate their thinking and decision-making instead
- Provide positive feedback and/or get them to reflect and recall their own success

As a mentor develop **TRUST:**

- Build rapport with the mentee every time you speak to re-establish the relationship
- Remind them that conversations are confidential and keep confidences
- Be willing to disclose (appropriate) information about yourself to show you trust them

Every relationship depends on trust. It doesn't matter whether it is spouses or colleagues, a family or a team, the level of trust strongly influences success.

Some of what develops or destroys trust is emotional and some is rational, so we need to work on both. There is a trust zone that is a culmination of several areas: Credibility, Reliability, Mutuality and Reciprocity.

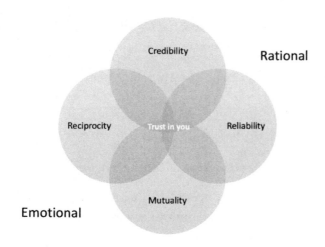

Figure 15: Trust Zone

CREDIBILITY: **I can believe you**

Those we consider trustworthy typically share some characteristics that allow them to establish credibility with us. We believe in their:

Integrity — they are honest and congruent. They do not lie. Their words and deeds match, they "walk the talk". They act in alignment with the values they espouse.

Capability — knowledge, skills, abilities that inspire our confidence. They know what they are talking about, their information is reliable. They have experience in their field.

RELIABILITY: **I can count on you**

For us to judge someone as reliable it's not enough to look good, they must fulfil the promise, summed up in the saying: "the proof of the pudding is in the eating" .

Performance — producing results. Getting things done. Doing the right things that make for effectiveness. meet expectations.

Consistency — dependable. They turn up, meet commitments.

MUTUALITY: **You *and* I benefit**

We are less reserved and more open with someone who shares their:

Intention — they show concern, they care about us, not just themselves and will act in our best interests. They strive for mutual benefit, not purely self-interest.

Motivation — straight-forward and transparent reasons. There is no hidden agenda.

Reciprocity: **You trust me**

Interestingly, you are more likely to get trust if you give trust.

Respect — acknowledge me as a person, my intelligence and autonomy and my right to be treated as an adult

Confidence — faith in my ability, belief I will do my part

Show you care and remember details they've shared. Show respect by giving your full attention and really listening. Apply the 80:20 principle, they should do 80% of the talking. Accept what they say, don't judge or criticise. Don't minimise or ridicule their feelings. You can show you trust them with appropriate self-disclosure, for example, if you have experienced similar feelings, but don't dominate the conversation and make it seem to be all about you rather than them.

Build the mentee's self-confidence by helping them:

- Find examples of their success in the past. This could include obstacles overcome, problems resolved or difficult situations that they got through.
- Make a list of positive achievements, review and add to it often.
- Help them set appropriate and achievable new goals.

When mentees are in a safe space, they will take the risk of self-disclosure and open to the possibility of exploring and setting goals. This can inspire a spiral of success that you can foster and build. The process enables an incremental and realistic expansion of the mentee's self-image as an achiever.

5

A FRAMEWORK FOR THE MENTORING CONVERSATION

Increasingly, mentoring is integral to a leader's role and many organisations have mentoring programs. Yet most mentoring happens in informal relationships, as a series of ad hoc meetings or casual conversations.

Few people are properly trained to lead mentoring conversations, but you can learn to lead a mentoring conversation with the simple and easy to remember framework I will spell out here. You will have the flexibility to adapt easily to any mentoring situation and you'll have confidence because you'll know what to say or ask next.

You don't have to have the title mentor to lead a mentoring conversation, but you do need to understand how to help people create insight and empower them to act on it.

In a work setting you might use mentoring conversations with individuals for career development, performance feedback or building capability. You can use them with teams talking about goals and outcomes, to plan or debrief projects, or to manage or adapt to change. You can also use this type of conversation in spontaneous mentoring moments that present themselves.

You can also lead mentoring conversations with friends, family, colleagues or employees when a mentoring moment presents itself. You can watch the lightbulb go on as they get that flash of insight and you can observe or assist as they decide what to do with it.

Mentoring relationships and conversations are not static, they are dynamic. They move and change because they are flexible and adapt to the person and the situation. There's no "one size fits all" or rigid formula.

Traditionally, we've thought about mentors as "wise guides" who share their knowledge and experience. While this is often useful, contemporary mentoring *begins* with a mentor asking questions and listening to a mentee. Mentoring is about offering support — encouraging and validating them, but it's also about sometimes challenging them by offering a different perspective. This is not an either/or decision; rather, you can think of it as a spectrum. You will elicit AND impart, support AND challenge and move along the spectrum as needed.

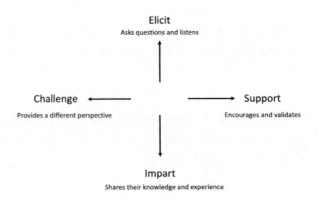

Figure 16: The Mentoring Dynamic

I developed the framework for a mentoring conversation based on adult learning, action learning, and classic principles of strategic planning. I call it a framework because, like when you build a house, you start with a secure foundation, in mentoring that is the safe space of trust and rapport (see previous chapter). Then you put in place a framework for the walls and roof. Once the foundations and framework are in place, you can go ahead and build the house, decorate the interior and create the home to suit the people.

As you'll see in the diagram below, I've laid the framework for a mentoring conversation out like an analog clock-face, where we begin at the twelve o'clock position. We'll generally move in a clockwise fashion, first getting the person to reflect on their current reality, the situation, issue, or topic they want to discuss. Then we discuss the future and help them make informed decisions about it. We may then assist them to set goals and plan actions. Finally, we'll support them as they take action.

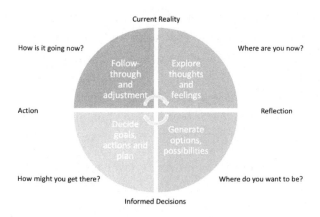

Figure 17: Framework for the Mentoring Conversation

Although I've suggested a clockwise cycle through this process, and I'll continue that as I explain each of the four stages in more detail, keep in mind that in a real mentoring conversation you'll likely skip back and forth many times. And, although I talk about the mentoring conversation, it is more likely to be a series of conversations over time.You can't rush it and you need to remain flexible! This is about enabling people to make decisions and set goals that are right for them. The framework provides a supporting structure for you and for them. I built it on four questions. These are not the questions you ask the mentee, but the questions you hold in your mind to frame the questions appropriate to the person and the situation. I call them the "Umbrella Questions"

1. Where are you now?
2. Where do you want to be?
3. How might you get there
4. How are you doing now?

WHERE ARE YOU NOW?

In the noon to three o'clock position, we want the mentee to explore their thoughts and feelings about the topic of the conversation. We want them to reflect; we want to draw them out. If we are successful, they will literally think out loud. Essentially, what you're trying to find out is "Where are you now?" You want the mentee to reflect on what's going on and clearly understand the current reality, problem, situation or event.

In the early stage of the mentoring conversation, we want to explore their thoughts and feelings. We're going to use open-ended questions, and start with very broad enquiries e.g. "What's on your mind today?" "What would you like to talk about? Later we can home in on the issue. It's really useful to train your mentees to send an agenda prior to the meeting. This will help them focus, help you prepare and ensure you both make best use of your time.

It is quite possible that when they reflect on the situation, they'll realise that there are deeper issues that need to be considered. The question on top of their mind may not be the actual issue. Freud said:

"The mind is like an iceberg, it floats with one-seventh of its bulk above water." There's a lot going on below the surface of the conscious mind. We are NOT trying to psychoanalyse our mentee, but we do want to increase their awareness of their own values, priorities, preferences and motivation.

We want them to talk, so we'll listen and use minimal responses like "mm hm", "uh huh", "go on" to encourage them to keep going. We might need to probe gently with phrases like "Can you say a little more about ..." "Would you expand on that ..." "Perhaps you'd like to say a little more about ..." And, at times we'll use reflective listening to help them clarify their thoughts, to check our understanding or summarise: "It sounds like you ..." "So, what you're saying is ..." "What I'm hearing is ..."

In this type of reflective conversation, the mentee may discover their own insights. You may see the lightbulb go on as they have that "ah ha!" moment. Have you ever had that? A sudden blinding flash of the obvious, or a slower dawning realisation? Maybe an actual epiphany! Sometimes that's all you need. It galvanizes you into action.

Maybe, by simply by listening, your job as a mentor is done!

Where Do You Want to Be?

You want to ensure that your mentee makes informed decisions about what they do. After all, Archimedes is said to have yelled "Eureka" and run naked out into the street after a flash of insight gave him the answer to a problem while he was in the bath! Insight generates excitement and energy, but we don't want enthusiasm to overrule good sense.

Also, some mentees may not know what they really want or what they're capable of. So, our job is to help them generate options and possibilities. Therefore, after establishing where they are now, we want to move to: "where do they want to be?"

You want to compare and contrast the current situation with the ideal one. You will continue using open questions, minimal responses, perhaps gentle probing, and reflective listening. But now we have an additional aim, we want them to make informed decisions before they take action.

If we go back to the Mentoring Dynamic (Figure # above), this could be a time where you share some of your own knowledge and experience. Or, it could be a time when you suggest they do some research for themselves, or perhaps use a self-assessment instrument like Strengths Finder to open up more possibilities.

How Might You Get There?

When they are well informed and ready, the conversation proceeds so that they can decide on their goals and plan actions. The umbrella question, having asked: where are you now, and where do you want to be, is: how might you get there? You'll guide them as they determine realistic ways forward, perhaps with a time-frame and measures of success.

How Are You Doing Now?

It will be sometime later, when they have had a chance to do something based on the conversation, that they'll come back so you can talk about follow-through and adjustment. You'll lead a review of the action and outcomes. The question that frames that conversation is: how are you doing now?

If you can remember these four questions, you'll never have to worry about what to say or do next. It will always be a variation of one of these questions. You want most of the planning to come from the mentee themselves. So as much as possible, keep asking them questions. Limit but don't withhold your own input. Don't be afraid to send them away with research tasks or let them go away to think about what you've spoken about and come back to you with ideas to discuss.

I'm sure you can immediately see the application of the mentoring conversation framework to a career development conversation. The early meetings would help the mentee identify values, priorities, preferences, and strengths. The Activities section of this book includes many activities you could get mentees to do to before setting goals and creating an action plan.

The key to a mentoring conversation is to remember that it is a dialogue, a two-way process. It involves creating a safe space of trust and rapport, asking good questions, listening well and not jumping in too quickly with advice or solutions.

6

DEVELOP TALENTS AND STRENGTHS

I guess I'm biased, but everything in my 40+ years in adult learning, career development and mentoring, convinces me that every one of us has more talent than we know. If you believe in mentoring, you believe that too. I've never met a person who didn't have untapped potential, more to give, more to learn and more to enjoy. I trained as a Gallup Strengths Coach and that has reinforced my belief.

Mentors can use career conversations to help people identify and develop their talents and strengths, so in this chapter I'll outline why strengths development is so important, what talents and strengths are, and how you, as a mentor can lead people to realise their potential.

WHY DEVELOP TALENTS AND STRENGTHS?

Based on the Gallup organisation's extensive world-wide research, we know that:

- People who use their strengths at work are more engaged. People who are engaged love their work, speak positively about their organisation and perform above and beyond expectations. Using strengths intrinsically motivates them.

- As organisations have moved to capability frameworks, we've found that developing capability fits very well with a strengths-based approach that encourages employees to take responsibility for developing their potential and productivity.
- Understanding individual strengths and differences, complementary and dynamic combinations with team-members and the strengths of the team itself is empowering.
- There's something within us that calls us to develop natural talents and there is joy in answering that call.
- It invigorates you when you use your strengths. Learning is quicker, easier, more enjoyable and you are more engaged and likely to experience "flow". Excellent performance is fulfilling.
- People who use their strengths every day are 12.5% more productive. That means they get more done, but work no harder.
- Using strengths feels good and makes you stronger. When you are strong, you can take challenges in your stride, you are less susceptible to stress.
- People working with their strengths look forward to going to work, have more positive than negative interactions with co-workers, treat customers better, tell their friends they work for a great employer, achieve more daily and have more positive, creative and innovative moments.
- When you are the best you can be, you contribute the most to work, life, community and the world.

What Are Talents and Strengths?

Most people who want to can work hard, learn and practice so that they reach an acceptable standard in the role you have hired them for. If they can't, you need to reassess your recruitment and selection process. However, excellence in any field is more likely to be achieved by those who have and develop a natural talent for it. Most of us can run, but few will ever become champion runners. Many can write, yet scarcely any are best-selling authors. Everyone can do simple addition, but a minority are mathematicians.

Talents usually mean that we have a natural predisposition for something and enjoy it so much that we do it frequently enough to become good at it. Talents are things that come easily and naturally to us. They come with the package of our body, brain and personality. They are raw materials, a natural part of you. You are born with talents and they stay with you throughout life.

You build talents into strengths by adding **knowledge, skills, and experience.** Like building a muscle, you must use knowledge and practice skills to become strong.

Knowledge is information that you gain and understand. You recall it when you need to, or internalise it so that you use it without even thinking about it.

Skill is the ability you develop, the techniques you learn, the know how that comes from practice.

Experience is what you get when you practice, hands on, the techniques, the craft. Writers hone their talent by writing, painters by painting. The same applies to bakers and plumbers, actors, physicians, teachers, engineers, cleaners and in any other field.

Some of us have developed one or two strengths but as someone once said: "If all you have is a hammer, it's tempting to treat everything like a nail". So, what we want to do is see what other tools we have in the kit and learn how to use them. This is especially important in the dynamic and fast-changing workplace of today.

Hidden Talent

Some of your talents are clear to you. If you stop and think about it, you can identify things you seem to be naturally good at. Some of your talents may be clear to others. They can point out things you do well, but some of your natural ability may not be visible to others. And, you have undiscovered potential that you don't know is there and others don't either.

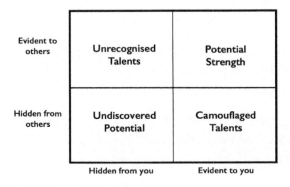

Figure 18: Talent Matrix

Unrecognised Talents

Your inborn talents pull you toward activities that let you use, develop and enjoy them. It is likely that others see your ability, just as you can recognise the "green thumb", the great cooking or craft skills of those around you. However, often people don't see their own talents. Talents remain unrecognised by you because they are so natural. Things that seem normal to you and come so easily to you that you think: "anyone could do that" are hard for you to recognise as talents.

Undiscovered Potential

Talent is raw material lying dormant with in you, it could remain undiscovered forever. It's like gold, you might be lucky enough to stumble upon it by being in the right place at the right time (I was, when I walked into a training room for the first time and knew I wanted to be out front) but usually, searching for gold requires you to know what you're looking for and use the right tools.

Camouflaged Talents

Spots on leopards, stripes on zebras and patterns on lizards conceal them in their environment. Many animals, insects and plants are masters of camouflage and are nearly invisible to others unless you look really hard. Talents can blend in with the background. They may be less visible to others because they are so much a part of the patterns of behaviour you exhibit. They're unnoticed, a part of what you do that allows you to do it well, but they don't stand out. Because of a lack of attention, it's possible that these talents are under-developed and under-utilised.

Potential Strengths

Identified talents are potential strengths. They may still need to be developed to reach full potential.

How to Recognise Talents

The best way to discover talents is with an objective assessment.

I've been using the CliftonStrengths Assessment for several years and I've found it invaluable in mentoring programs, team development workshops and individual coaching and mentoring.

You can purchase it for yourself online [1]from the Gallup Strengths Center:

The fee for doing CliftonStrengths Assessment provides detailed personalised reports, videos and other information to understand and develop your talents. Or, you can buy a hard copy book which comes with a code for the online instrument.

There are other ways to recognise your talents because our natural born temperament is like a magnet that pulls us to develop the raw ingredients nature provided. You may feel:

- **Magnetic attraction:** you sense a "calling" to a vocation, yearning to do particular things, a strong inclination toward some aspects of your job.
- **Rapid Learning:** you have a knack for doing certain things. You quickly pick up techniques and it's easy and enjoyable to learn because you are very interested and can't get enough of the topic.
- **Instinctive Response:** you recognise the things you naturally do well. Perhaps you're a strategic thinker, a people person, a good influencer, or you just get things done.
- **Immense Satisfaction:** certain aspects of your work thrill you, perhaps it's solving problems, organising events, negotiating a great deal or helping others grow. That's your thing.

One way to develop an awareness of talents and strengths is through personal reflection; another is through feedback. A third is with a psychometric instrument. The best way is to combine all three. I have included activities you can offer your mentee to help them identify talents.

If you have not taken the CliftonStrengths Assessment, you might consider doing so. It will open a whole new world of development opportunities for you and allow you to better mentor others.

How to Develop **Strengths**

To turn talents into strengths, we need the opportunity—the chance to develop. We also need to invest time and energy in building talents so they truly become strengths. This is why I say that I never met a person who did not have more potential and more to contribute. Often, we have not had the awareness or the opportunity, or we may not have invested in developing our strengths.

Strengths fall into one of four categories:

1. **You think about information and situations:** How do you mentally navigate your world? Do you have a focus on the future or an interest in the past? Is your preference to analyse data or situations? Perhaps you love to learn, reflecting and drawing the lesson from events? Maybe you consume and absorb information, collecting facts and interesting ideas? You're one who seeks what you need to make better decisions?

2. **You make things happen:** Are you a get-it-done type of person? Disciplined and focussed? Prepared to take responsibility? You jump in to fix things? Driven by a purpose? You are good at organising others? You like to work out the steps? Pursue goals?

3. **You influence others:** Do you take charge? Motivate? Thrive on competition? Communicate well? Are you self-confident

and persuasive? You always look for improvement? Want to be known for some significant contribution?

4. **You build and maintain relationships:** Are you a people-person? Find it easy to empathise with others? Inclusive, making all feel welcomed? Flexible and able to tailor your approach to a person's uniqueness? Do you love to help people develop? See the bright side of situations?

The Gallup organisation has been researching effectiveness in the workplace for decades. It has defined 34 talent themes across these four areas as: Strategic Thinking, Executing, Influencing and Relationship Building. We need all four domains in effective teams. Individuals may have dominant strengths in one, two, three or all four.

Developing talents and strengths is integral to career conversations in mentoring. It will make your mentoring joyful and rewarding, so I recommend it as an area for you to learn more about and you'll find a wealth of resources on the Gallup website.

PART III

CAREER CONVERSATIONS

This is the in-depth guide to each of the four steps of a mentoring conversation focussed on career. Each chapter suggests what to aim for as a mentor and what the outcomes for the mentee will be, then provides a précis of useful topics to discuss, and the activities to support your conversations. We take the four questions at the heart of the framework and expand them.

Where Are You Now? Helps the mentee take stock of current personal and work issues and review their past experiences with self-assessment and reflection.

Where Do You Want to Be? Gets them exploring future possibilities and examining options.

How Might You Get There? Guides them to make informed decisions, set goals and create their action plans.

How's it Going Now? This important chapter is about follow-through and adjustment as you review progress with them. It also looks at dealing with difficulties and the reality of failure and how to handle success.

7

WHERE ARE YOU NOW?

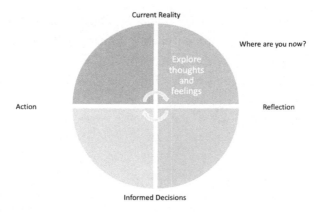

Figure 19: Framework for a Mentoring Conversation —
Where are you now?

In the early stages of a career conversation, you will want to build trust and rapport so that the mentee feels confident to open up about their thoughts and feelings. This part of the conversation includes exploring how work affects the mentee's life and the people and things they care about.

You want to help the mentee take stock of where they are, look at what satisfies them and what does not, think about their motivation and interests, and decide what is important to them at work and life.

Aims

You will lead conversations that enable the mentee to:

- Explore interests, preferences and motivation
- Identify values, and principles and life goals
- Recognise strengths, talents, skills and personal attributes
- Define areas for further development
- List practical considerations when planning career actions.

Outcomes

As a result the mentee will have:

- Decision-making criteria on which to base career choices
- Data to be used in their career portfolio and resumé
- A foundation for a professional development plan
- Potential career goals for further investigation

Useful Topics to Discuss

- Values
- Meaning and Purpose at Work
- Job Satisfaction
- Strengths
- Transferrable Skills
- Capabilities

Values

Personal values, the ideals or standards you regard as most important, influence decisions about life. For example you may value freedom and live a lifestyle that allows you not to become "too tied down"; in contrast, you could value stability and security and build your life around achieving that. No-one can say that either of these approaches is right or wrong, they are individual value-judgements. Your values have developed over a lifetime and are slow to change. If you make a decision or take action that contradicts your value-system you are likely to feel discomfort until realignment occurs.

Values play a major part in job and career satisfaction. The match between a person's values and the degree to which a role meets them can range from zero to one hundred percent. Career values provide criteria for making career decisions and evaluating job options. Values influence such issues as:

- Where you want to live and work
- What kind of is job appealing
- What kind of co-workers you work best with
- What working conditions suit you
- What level of responsibility you feel comfortable handling
- What income level is important to attain

ACTIVITIES TO AID **conversations about career values:**

- Values Discovery Worksheet
- Meeting Values
- Heroes Hall of Fame
- Tools for Mentoring Video 4. Personal Values

Meaning and Purpose at Work

There is a fundamental human need for meaning and purpose. Without it, life seems worthless and work is boring and pointless.

What makes work meaningful and gives a sense of purpose is different for different individuals, but the vast majority of employees seek fulfilment from their job. PwC[1] found 83% of employees rated meaning in day-to-day work as the most important factor in their current job. People need to feel that their contribution has value, they want to make a difference and what they do is important.

Employees may gain meaning and purpose from the mission of the organisation — the products or services it provides, reinforced by the culture — if they can link that to the work they do, see how they fit in, and that what they do matters. They can also find meaning and purpose in their occupation. When they do the work is intrinsically rewarding, they are more engaged, motivated, productive and happy.

People who find meaning and purpose in their work are more resilient. However, should they lose their job, or retire without other avenues of fulfilment, their wellbeing will suffer.

Organisations have mission statements, some families and individuals do too. A mission guides goal setting and decision-making and reduces stress. It helps set direction instead of being pulled off-course like a rudderless ship. Walt Disney's famous personal mission was: "To make people happy" today, the huge corporation defines its mission as: "to entertain, inform and inspire people around the globe through the power of unparalleled storytelling, reflecting the iconic brands, creative minds and innovative technologies that make ours the world's premier entertainment company."

A personal mission statement will help your mentee find meaning and purpose in the work they do, or look for a role where they are more likely to be fulfilled. A modified version of a mission statement is useful on a resumé and in job interviews. Their mission will reflect their values, priorities and personal aspirations.

. . .

Activities to aid **conversations about meaning and purpose**

- Write a Personal Mission Statement
- Tools for Mentoring Video 3 Personal Strategic Planning

Job Satisfaction

Job satisfaction is more and more important to whether people stay or leave a job, and it should be a major consideration when choosing a new role. Finding out what does and does not satisfy your mentee is a critical part of career self-appraisal.

Pay and benefits are important to workers, after all most of us "work for a living". We all have living expenses, bills to pay, and want to have money to save or spend on discretionary items. If people believe they are well paid they are more likely to be satisfied than if they are poorly paid. But salaries are far from the only factors affecting job satisfaction, as shown below.

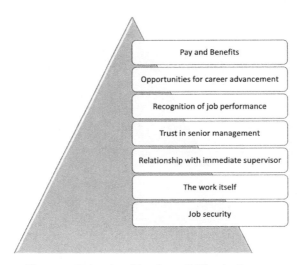

Figure 20: University of Southern California, Reasons
Employees are Unhappy

People are more satisfied and productive when work is aligned with their interest and preferences and has the right amount of challenge. Too little challenge will leave them bored; too much challenge will cause stress and overwhelm.

Some elements of job satisfaction are out of an employee's control, such as how well leadership communicates with employees, but some they can influence themselves. You can help them become more proactive in seeking career development opportunities, up-skilling, getting feedback etc. Or, you can ensure they look for elements of job satisfaction in the role, and the culture and leadership style of a new workplace.

The COVID-19 pandemic in 2020 saw many people forced to work from home. Many like it and want to keep the flexibility of at least part of the week outside the office. 2020 also saw people re-evaluate their priorities and the relative importance of work and personal life. Mental health and wellbeing also took a battering and people are more conscious of the need to look for ways to preserve it for themselves and their loved ones. These factors also feed into job satisfaction.

. . .

Activities to aid **conversations about job satisfaction:**

- Career to Date
- Preferences
- Three Dimensional Analysis
- Tools for Mentoring Video 5: 3D Career Development

Strengths

As discussed in Chapter 6, we should base career conversations on helping people identify and develop their talents and strengths. Use that information to lead conversations about why strengths development is important, what talents and strengths are, and how discovering their strengths will help them realise their potential.

Activities to aid **conversations about strengths**

- Strengths Discovery
- Strengths 30 Day Challenge
- Tools for Mentoring Video 6. Discover Your Strengths

Transferrable Skills

Transferrable skills are those you can use in many different roles. The mentee needs to appraise their transferrable skills because this gives them lots more options when considering career moves.

Transferrable skills are portable. They include technical skills such as coding or data analysis, human skills such as teamwork and communication, as well as personal attributes like adaptability and resilience.

Recruiters will use many transferrable skills as keywords and they need to appear in applicant's resumés for them to be considered. Some transferrable skills are in high demand, and you should get the mentee to research the most current lists so that they can identify those they have and those they may need to develop.

- Growth Mindset – wants to learn
- Continuous Learning – hones and builds new skills
- Critical Thinking – innovative problem-solving
- Survival Skills – adaptability, grit
- Resilience, Curiosity – easily adjust
- Flexibility – comfortable with change
- Dedication – turning up, despite challenges
- Coaching Mindset – help others learn
- Versatility - comfort with ambiguity
- Thriving in a Virtual Environment

Figure 21: Forbes Human Resource Council Expert Panel The Top 10 Skills Recruiters Are Looking For In 2021.

It is also beneficial for the mentee to identify their motivated skills and prioritise these when researching their options. Motivated skills are those things that they are good at and enjoy doing. They are the skills most likely to bring them satisfaction and success in their career. In your conversations, get the mentee to talk about work and non-work activities and accomplishments that they did well, are proud of, or enjoy most. Help them recognise the skills they used in these to include in their skills audit.

ACTIVITIES TO AID **conversations about transferrable skills**

- Skills Audit
- Functional Skills Checklist
- Personal Attributes Checklist
- Turn Personal Attributes into Skills
- Transferrable Skills
- Motivated Skills

CAPABILITIES

Capabilities include knowledge and abilities as well as skills necessary for various roles. NSW government agencies have developed A Capability Framework[2] that describes twenty capabilities organised into five categories: Personal Attributes, Relationships, Results, Business Enablers and People Management plus Occupational Specific capability sets for specialist, technical or trade-related roles, with five levels from Foundational to Highly Advanced.

In Australia, most government agencies and organisations have adopted a capability framework for workforce management. Even if the mentee has no intention of working in the public sector, it's worth understanding the concept because:

- The Capability Framework demonstrates capabilities are transferrable from one role to another
- The five generic capability areas expand the mentee's ability to self-appraise as they recognise their own skills and abilities
- The Capability Framework shows the value of human skills ("Relationships" is a required category for every role) and personal attributes
- The Framework shows that there are many valued, generic

(transferrable) capabilities compared to occupational specific capabilities
- Capabilities more fully describe what they require for roles
- Using The Capability Framework (freely available to download[3] online) you can help the mentee see that they may have many more options for career moves with the capabilities they have
- The levels for each capability allow discussions with the mentee about skills and abilities they may want to develop
- The Framework describes capabilities in language that recruiters are familiar with and mentees may need to lear

ACTIVITIES TO AID conversations about Capabilities

- Analyse Your Capabilities

Additional Resources:

The Capability Framework[4] (NSW) or the equivalent in your location or, if your own organisation has something similar, use that.

PUTTING it All Together

By completing some or all of the activities suggested in this chapter, your mentee will have compiled a lot of information. Now they need to put it together in a useful format to use as they move forward. With your assistance they can prepare:

- A Career Portfolio
- Areas for Development

There are checklists/templates for each of these in the Activities section of this book. Mentees should regard each of these documents as a work-in-progress to review and revise as necessary. They may want to modify the documents as they complete activities in the next chapters.

A Career Portfolio

This might be a ring binder with plastic sleeves, a file-box with a series of folders, or a folder with files on a computer. Whatever format suits your mentee, their career portfolio contains all relevant information about their career it will contain items such as:

- Career goals
- List of competences
- List of achievements
- Resumé and/or curriculum vitae
- Certificates, diplomas, degrees, awards
- Job descriptions
- Performance appraisals
- References or letters of recommendation or compliments
- Record of training, development and education
- Samples of work
- List of previous supervisors
- Referees with their current contact details
- Any other relevant documentation

Areas for Development

As the mentee reflected on their talents, strengths, skills and capabilities, it will have become clear that they have some scope to further develop them. This may or may not be a priority but it is useful to list potential areas for development on the template provided. They can use this in later conversations with you, or in conversations with their manager about their professional development.

The activities in this chapter are a sizeable piece of work. Hopefully, the mentee has gained insight as well as information that they can use. They deserve congratulations on their efforts.

8

WHERE DO YOU WANT TO BE

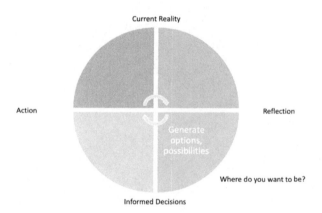

Figure 22: Framework for a Mentoring Conversation —
Where do you want to be?

One of the major benefits you can offer your mentee is expanding their awareness. The last chapter was about ways to increase their self-awareness; this one turns their gaze outwards to possibilities for their future.

You want to empower them and you can do that by helping them see the options and choices that are available to them.

Aims

You will lead conversations that enable the mentee to:

- Explore possibilities
- Identify and realistically assess their options
- Draft a career aim

Outcomes

Analysing and discussing the information they gather will give them:

- Greater awareness of opportunities
- Confirmation or adjustments of aspirations
- Information on which to base decisions

Useful Topics to Discuss

- Beliefs About What's Possible
- Research Methods
- Seven Potential Career Moves
- Career Aims

BELIEFS About What's Possible

It is likely that your mentee will have some beliefs about what is and isn't possible for them. Beliefs are thoughts, opinions, ideas, or assumptions that may or may not be accurate. Occasionally, a person will have an inflated opinion of their ability. Sometimes, people have well-founded self-confidence. More frequently, people underestimate their capabilities and potential. Imposter syndrome is common, particularly amongst women achievers who think "eventually, they are going to realise I'm not as smart as they think". Such beliefs limit their horizons and lower their self-worth.

Mentees may not express limiting beliefs overtly, because most are unconscious. You may just sense a hesitancy, or perhaps a resistance to change, but be alert for comments like: "I'm too old/young", "I could never do that", or "I'm not that smart" or other comments that imply they are, in some way, not good enough.

Often, we base beliefs about what is possible on limited or incorrect information. That's why you'll get the mentee to do research, but you may also need to help them dissolve beliefs or fears based only on what they or others have said. Parents, teachers, friends or complete strangers can inadvertently inject thoughts into an impressionable mind. It is easy to absorb negative comments or criticism received as a child, or at any stage, that reverberate throughout life via a judgemental inner critic. The inner critic is a form of negative self-talk that reinforces limiting beliefs, and undermines confidence to make positive changes in their life.

Update Beliefs	
I'm too old/young	It might be a challenge for someone my age, but others have, and I can too
I'm not smart enough	I'd need to develop the knowledge and skills for that
I'm a failure	I had a go, and it didn't work out, but here's what I learned
I'm no good at ...	It will be a steep learning curve
I can't ...	I haven't yet

Figure 23: Update Beliefs

Since this part of the mentoring conversation is about generating options and possibilities, if limiting beliefs are holding them back, you'll want to help them shift their perspective. In terms of The Mentoring Dynamic (see chapter?) this involves balancing elicit and support with impart and challenge. You'll need to have developed rapport and trust and walk the path gently and respectfully as you lead this type of conversation. A mentee with an inner critic doesn't need another on the outside, and if they become defensive, it will be a barrier to communication.

Essentially, your aim is to enable them to recognise and take pride in their capabilities and have faith in their potential. You can help them realise that beliefs and the thoughts and opinions of their inner critic are not always reality. They can change negative self-talk to something more constructive, and old beliefs can be updated.

Modify Self-Talk	
I always …	Sometimes I … but now I'll …
I'll never …	I haven't tried … yet
I can't …	I don't know if I can … yet
I must …	I might …
I should …	I could …
Everyone knows …	Some people might think …
It's awful	It's inconvenient/upsetting
That would be terrible	That's not my preferred outcome

Figure 24: Modify Self-talk

A person can reduce the effects of an inner critic, limiting beliefs and negative self-talk by:

- Recognising the inner critic in action - call it out
- Using rational thinking to evaluate how much truth is, or is not, in the criticism

- Choosing more constructive ways to self-critique for self-improvement
- Practicing compassion (for others and one's self)
- Learning to change self-talk

Develop your own repertoire of questions and phrases to use in this type of conversations. Here are some samples:

"Sounds like you may have an over-active inner critic giving you a hard time?"

"It that really true, or something your inner critic tells you?"

"Perhaps that was so in the past, but could it be different in the future?"

"Can I ask, what led you to that conclusion?"

"I'm curious to know what prompted that opinion?"

"I'm wondering if there's another way to look at that?"

"Isn't that a bit harsh? How would a good friend more kindly give you that feedback?"

"Self-critique can be useful for improvement, but criticism seldom is. How could you think about that in a more constructive way?"

People can update beliefs about what's possible by seeking examples from the real world. Ordinary people do extraordinary things all the time. Many successful people and high achievers come from humble beginnings. You may tell parts of your own story, if it is appropriate, or you may point to examples of people known to you, or have the mentee research the biography of people who achieved in areas they are interested in.

ACTIVITIES TO AID **conversations about beliefs:**

- Deal With Your Inner Critic

- Self-critique for Self-Improvement
- Update Beliefs About Yourself
- Myth-Busting

RESEARCH METHODS

Because we want mentees to make informed decisions, it is imperative that they get information about potential moves from reliable sources. You can talk to them about:

- Checking pre-requisites for potential occupations
- Collecting information from a variety of sources
- Networking and interviewing for information

We're not at the job application phase yet, simply exploring options, so it's important to look broadly at possibilities. People looking for a career move can prematurely rule themselves out of an opportunity by assuming they don't have the prerequisites for a particular role. So have your mentee gather some role descriptions and job advertisements so you can discuss the difference between essential criteria — the must-haves, qualifications or experience required, and desirable criteria — aspects that are an advantage, but won't rule out a suitable applicant. Obviously, an applicant needs the right qualifications for specific professions, but an exceptional candidate can bypass even some essential criteria. Someone with a certificate or a diploma sometimes gets by where recruiters ask for a degree. Help your mentee understand that while employers expect a new person to do the job for which they hired them, there is room for learning and development in any role.

Of course, the mentee will search online for information about occupations of interest and organisations. Again, they want to search broadly, not rely on a single source. They can look at social media, news publications, and industry associations, educational institutions, as well as an organisation's own website. If the mentee is looking at specific occupations, they should find out about likely remuneration and the implications of that for them. High-paid roles are more competitive, low-paid ones may satisfy but may not provide sufficient income. They also have to consider the cost and time necessary for any training and education in a new field.

The best source of information remains word-of-mouth. They may reach out to people who work in the field or at the organisation for first-hand information. Encourage them to ask friends and family outside their current workplace if they know and can introduce them. LinkedIn can be a useful network. If they are looking within their own organisation, there will be people to talk to. Coach them in how to have these conversations and/or have them research for articles on networking and interviewing for information and the etiquette of doing so.

Seven Potential Career Moves

Many people want career advancement. They hope or expect to get promoted or move to a higher pay grade regularly. However, with flatter organisational structures, project-based work and teams, this may not be available and roles and the skills in demand change. People will have to re-skill or change their skill-set many times over their work-life. What we once thought of as a career ladder must now become a Career Lattice. Like lattice used in a garden, a career lattice is a sturdy framework that supports, protects and enables growth in many directions.

As a mentor, you can help broaden the mentee's scope for satisfaction at work by increasing their awareness of various career moves.

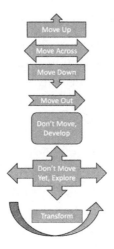

Figure 25: Seven Career Moves. Inspired by Beverly Kaye, Up Is Not the Only Way.

1. Move Up

It is still possible for some to move up in an organisation the traditional way people have progressed in the past, but it is not automatic. It depends upon them developing and enhancing their capabilities, being in an organisation that has such opportunities and being able to compete successfully against other applicants.

2. Move Across

Instead, a person may choose to gain broader experience by moving across to take a role that does not change their status or pay. This could make them more competitive for a future upward move, expose them to a new leader, different people and work, allow them to develop or expand skills and refresh their interest and enthusiasm.

3. Move Down

It is sometimes worth moving down to learn and grow in a different area, perhaps to launch a new career or profession, or for work-life balance. There are a growing number of parents unwilling to forgo important life events for the demands of their job, and it's not just women who feel the pressure of balancing parenthood and work[1].

4. Move Out

If there are no suitable opportunities, the culture is unsupportive or there is a lack of alignment of values, it may be necessary to move out of the organisation. I knew a woman who was an administrative assistant in a marketing department. She studied at night and gained a diploma, then a degree in marketing. However, she knew her employer would only ever see her as an assistant. She successfully applied elsewhere and achieved a role as a marketing manager in a different organisation.

Better pay and status, a shorter commute or a myriad of other benefits may be attractive. However, people should do their homework and make informed decisions before leaving one organisation for another, to avoid disappointment.

5. Don't Move, Develop

It is possible to overlook possibilities for increasing satisfaction within a current role. Looking for ways to grow, develop capabilities, do more of what they love, or include more interesting work in the job they're in. This is job enrichment. It may take some creativity to find ways they can use the strengths and motivated skills they identified earlier. And, it will require the cooperation of their leaders and maybe collaboration of team-members. However, as the productivity benefits of employee engagement through enabling them to use and develop their strengths at work becomes more widely known, good leaders will encourage this. It may also be a short-term solution.

6. Don't Move Yet, Explore

Similarly, a short-term strategy might be don't move, yet — explore. It may be necessary to continue to investigate potential career moves, or the chosen direction may need further planning, education or skills development. Some people take on a side-hustle, something they do free-lance or part-time as well as their day job, either to test the water, build up to a viable business or simply for the love of what they do out of hours.

7. Transform

Another option is to partially or totally transform their career. This might involve re-skilling, developing a different skill-set, an alternative career path through formal education, or starting their own business. Business start-up is a very specialised area, there will be financial issues, local laws, health and safety, compliance, bookkeeping and tax issues to master. Business start-up probably requires a mentor with expertise in both entrepreneurship and business management.

ACTIVITIES TO AID conversations about potential career moves

- Seven Career Moves
- Moving Up Checklist
- Lateral Move Checklist
- Downward Move Checklist
- Moving Out Checklist
- Don't Move - Develop
- Don't Move - Explore
- Transformation
- Options Exploration

CAREER AIMS

Your aim is to assist the mentee to make informed decisions about their future. So, now it's time to set goals. Unless there is an immediate opportunity that they are excited about, these goals will be general rather than specific, and be about the mentee rather than a particular role. Setting these goals draws on both the insights gained in their self-assessment and the information gathered in their research about potential career moves.

They should start with a broad career aim like:

"I'd like a role that allows me to use my strengths and capabilities such as... Where the nature of the work involves...

The work environment is...

That meets my highest priority lifestyle preferences of..."

ACTIVITIES TO AID **conversations about career aims**

- Dartboard
- The Clock
- Life Goals
- Career Aim

In the next chapter, How Might You Get There, you'll work with the mentee to refine and specify several goals to work towards, along with strategies and action plans to achieve them. For now, you want to take a holistic approach that helps them keep their personal priorities in the frame when they make decisions.

9

HOW MIGHT YOU GET THERE?

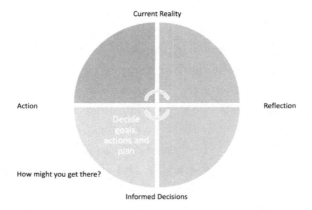

Figure 26: Framework for a Mentoring Conversation —
How might you get there?

Aims

You will lead conversations that enable the mentee to:

- Make informed decisions about their career direction

- Make a realistic assessment of obstacles
- Set their goals and plan the way forward

Outcomes

As a result, the mentee will have:

- Measurable goals and action plans to achieve them

Useful Topics to Discuss

- Making Career Decisions
- Career Constraints and Risks
- Goal Setting and Planning

Making Career Decisions

The simplest decision-making process is to list pros and cons, not because this is a reliable method, but because it is an easy starting point and conversation-starter. For example, my daughter once asked for my help to decide between two very different jobs offered to her. So I asked her to come have lunch with me and bring pen and paper to make a pro/con list. When we met, as soon as she started talking about the two jobs, I knew which one she wanted. It was in her glowing face, the way she spoke about it, and a dozen other non-verbal clues. However, there was some issue troubling her, preventing her from deciding. I gave no opinion, but had her draw a line down the centre of a page, put a plus sign on one side and a minus on the other, then make the list regarding the job she was most attracted to. She had only put a few words on the page when the real problem came up. Then we could have a conversation about that issue and make a plan for dealing with it. She accepted the job she really wanted, and it was a springboard for a very satisfying career path and a lot of fun!

For your mentee to make a sound decision, it needs to be based on the work they've done so far in identifying values, needs, wants, skills and potential.

Lead a conversation that first clarifies what the decision is. Are they thinking about quitting their job, exploring a particular option, taking a job offer, choosing between two directions, retraining, or creating a new long-term plan?

Next, help them check that their choice will meet their highest priorities. We frequently hear people say "this ticks all my boxes". Decision-making criteria are simply what's in those boxes for choosing one career direction over another. Have them review previous activities to list and rank what they will take into consideration when making their choice. One way to do this is divide their list into Must Haves, Want to Haves and Nice to Haves, then rank the Must Haves.

Must Haves	Want to Have	Nice to Have
1. Manager/leadership that encourages and supports me 2. Flexible (more than work from home) options 3. Meaningful, satisfying work 4. Salary range meets my expectations 5. Positive challenge and room for growth 6. Work/life balance 7. Productivity measures based on outcomes more than inputs	• Equity policies and practice • Opportunities for development • Diverse team of people I can be productive with • Employer is a good corporate citizen • Location that suits me • Up to date technology and systems • Employee Assistance Schemes (EAS) • Digital learning programs • Reskilling and upskilling as technology or needs change • Student loan repayment plan	• Subsidised study • Bonus for performance • Wellness benefits • Mental health support • Modern (culturally) workplace • Paid time off for volunteering

Figure 27: Example, Prioritised Decision Criteria

Ranking priorities is subjective and personal. For example, a few years ago I downsized my home and moved into an over fifty-fives lifestyle village. There are hundreds of such places in the state I live, and I spent months researching online. I visited many villages and looked at dozens of houses. I had a list of criteria to be ticked off, but my number one was a deal-breaker. If they did not meet this one, none of the others mattered — the village had to be pet friendly and allow me to keep my cats! It wasn't the only thing that made my mind up, of course. Location, the style of house, number of bedrooms, local facilities and services were important criteria too, but having all those factors clear and prioritised made my decision easy.

Activities to aid conversations about decision-making

- Priority Checklist
- Decision-Making Criteria

CAREER CONSTRAINTS and Risks

Before you let them firm up goals and action plans, a reality check is in order. Lead a conversation about their particular career constraints and the likely risks of the direction they have chosen. These constraints and risks do not mean they can't achieve their goals, only that ways of dealing with them must be part of their plan.

To identify constraints, the two of you can brainstorm a list of barriers, obstacles or problems that could be a hindrance to getting their goal. Then, list the factors that will help them and use the Force-Field Analysis to highlight issues they'll need to work on. Help them prioritise, set goals and create action plans to address each of these. Keep in mind that increasing the helping factors can be as useful as reducing the hindering forces.

These days, people may stay in a particular role for three or fewer years. So it is unlikely that a wrong move will prove disastrous in the longer term. However, it is worth minimising risk, having a fall-back position and a plan to manage a worst-case scenario.

To identify risks associated with particular career moves, consider the cost, personally, financially, socially and psychologically as well as unintended or potentially negative consequences. For example, further studies will cost them time and money, there could be implications for their personal relationships and a trade-off between this and other life goals. A shift to another role or organisation may not work out for many reasons. What would that mean for them? A downward move may bring loss of status and lower pay. How will that affect them?

Awareness of constraints and risks may be all that's necessary. Or, you may need to help them figure out ways to overcome constraints or minimise risks. Either way, it is better for them to have a realistic outlook.

Risk Management

Identify	What negative or unintended consequences could occur?
Prevent	What could you do that might prevent this happening?
Minimise	If you can't prevent it, what might reduce the impact?
Contingency Plan	If this happens, what will you do?

Figure 28: Risk Management

Classic risk management focuses first on ways to prevent the threat from eventuating. Then, looks at how to minimise the impact should the event occur, and finally, comes up with ways to deal with the worst-case scenario. So, once you have identified risks, start a conversation about how they could reduce the chance of negative consequences, reduce negative effects and contingency plans.

ACTIVITIES TO AID **conversations about career constraints and risk**

- Force-Field Analysis
- Risk Management
- Plan Plan Z

GOAL SETTING **and Planning**

Your mentee has set a broad career aim and some life goals. Now it is
time to set more specific goals and plan actions to achieve them. It is
useful to think of this as a hierarchy of goals.

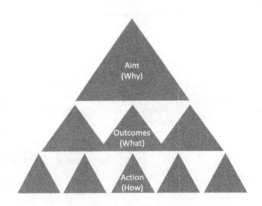

Figure 25: Hierarchy of Goals

An **aim** is very broad, but it is important. It describes where they're
headed and why it's important. It provides the purpose for their

effort, the reason why they chose this direction. Think of it as an overarching mission that they will fulfil.

Outcomes describe what needs to be done to achieve the aim. They break down the mission into strategies that will enable them to achieve their aspiration. These are specific and measurable goals.

Actions specify how to achieve the outcomes. These detail what they will do, when, and the resources necessary to implement the actions that will move them toward their goals.

It is likely that the high-level aim will take some time to achieve. So you need to discuss a realistic timeframe for each outcome with your mentee. Help them place the actions on a timeline, with a focus on what they can do immediately and the sequence or priorities that follow.

It will be helpful for the mentee to create an action plan that allows them to track progress. They could use planning or project management software, an app, a spreadsheet or the simple template provided. Whatever works for them is OK, it just needs to consolidate and map out what they will do, when, to achieve the outcomes they've specified. Ticking off tasks is surprisingly satisfying and motivating in any project and is especially important for achieving long-term goals.

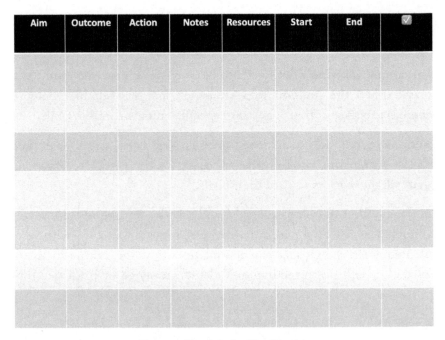

Aim	Outcome	Action	Notes	Resources	Start	End	☑

Figure 30: Simple Action Plan Template

ACTIVITIES TO AID **conversations about goals**

- Goal Analysis
- Know Your Outcomes
- Action Plan

You and your mentee have worked hard to get to this point, but the job's not done yet! In some ways, what comes next is the most important part of mentoring. It is your ongoing support, guidance, feedback and encouragement that will be vital to their goal achievement.

10

HOW'S IT GOING NOW?

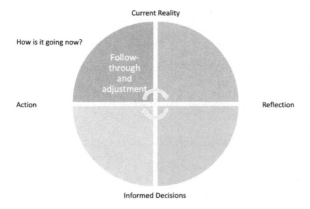

Figure 31: *Framework for a Mentoring Conversation — How's it going now?*

This part of the mentoring conversation is about the mentee's follow-through and adjustment. They are making purposeful changes which may not be easy. Your continued support and encouragement is vital. You will be someone they can rightfully share their successes with and also discuss challenges.

Don't expect the mentee's implementation of their plan to be flawless. There are some people who leap into action and continue until the job's done, but most of us are enthusiastic at the beginning, then life gets in the way, things don't go as hoped or unexpected obstacles appear. Your job is to help them follow through, deal with challenges, and adjust when necessary.

Aims:

You will lead conversations that enable mentees to:

- Review progress towards their goals
- Deal with difficulties and unforeseen events
- Adjust goals and plans if necessary

Outcomes:

As a result mentees will have:

- Motivation to complete tasks
- Growing self-confidence
- Satisfaction with accomplishments

Useful Topics to Discuss:

- Reviewing Progress
- Dealing With Difficulties
- There is No Success Without Failure
- How to Handle Success

Reviewing Progress

A longer-term goal needs milestones that let people know how they are progressing. Hopefully, you and your mentee did this as part of the goal setting and planning. If not, help your mentee figure out now what they can monitor to show that they are on track.

If your mentee is going well, positive feedback will encourage them, but don't let them rest on their laurels and become complacent. Help them keep their eyes on the prize. While you want them to take satisfaction in how far they've come, looking at what's still to be done is necessary to maintain motivation.

If the mentee is not doing so well, remind them that achieving goals is not easy; they're meant to be a stretch. Help them recognise what they have achieved so far. Self-doubt can rob a person of the grit to see the plan though, so take every opportunity to remind them of their strengths. Get them to talk about challenges that they've overcome in the past. Remind them they can increase their ability, learn new skills and gain new knowledge, and that practice and experience improve performance. Cite evidence from their background and history that they have shared with you previously.

Break big goals down into smaller steps. Stephen Guise, author of *Mini Habits - Smaller Habits, Bigger Results*, advocates breaking down goals into "stupid small" steps. For example, if your goal is to do ten push-ups, set a mini habit goal of one push-up. This YouTube video[1] explains the concept and the science behind it.

Make sure you continue to meet regularly, even if they say they have no progress to report. Talking with you helps keep their goals alive and there are always experiences they can learn from. Besides, just because you are working on a particular goal, doesn't mean that day-to-day development and growth don't matter. Your conversations will help them gain insights and learning from their life and work.

Conversations can be easy and non-threatening, yet very productive. Work and non-work issues can be relevant. Do a welfare check - how's their work/life balance going? Are they getting enough sleep/fun/time for family, or other important aspects of life? Refer to the Dartboard activity. Do they have other short-term goals?

. . .

USEFUL QUESTIONS FOR REVIEW SESSIONS:

"What's been happening, since we last met?"

"What's worked well for you? What didn't work out so well?"

"In hindsight, is there anything you could do differently?"

DEALING With Difficulties

If your mentee encounters difficulties, adopt a collaborative problem-solving approach.

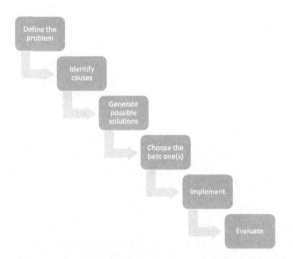

Figure 32: Classic Problem Solving

Often just talking it through with you as a sounding board will be enough for them to see what needs to be done. Listen closely and ask questions without offering solutions too quickly. Have them look back at their risk-management notes. Were these issues foreseen? What actions did they plan to deal with them?

However, before you work on solutions, it will be important to ensure you're working on the real problem. What doctors and counsellors call "the presenting problem" — the description of symptoms or issues — is not the root cause of their difficulties.

If progress has slowed or stalled, you'll need to lead a non-judgemental conversation about why that is so. To get to the root cause of a problem you may need to ask why several times, working through a chain of cause and effect issues. However, asking "why" can trigger defensiveness and justification. This can cause the mentee to focus on their fears, shortcomings or insecurities and it can entrench their mindset, keeping them stuck.

You're going to have to reduce the dangers of defensiveness. The three fundamental techniques for this are non-verbal, cushions and rephrasing why. Your non-verbal communication needs to convey respectful curiosity. Cushions are phrases that preface a confronting question. The words are a respectful way of asking permission to ask a question, combined with a gentle tone of voice and non-threatening body-language. You may even take the word *why* right out of the question by rephrasing.

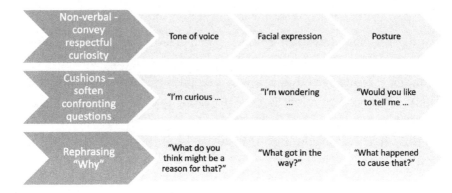

Figure 33: Reducing Defensiveness

Be alert to cues that it is not external obstacles that are holding them back, but some conflict within. It required commitment and continuous effort to achieve goals. Are they still committed to the goal?

Typical problems boil down to:

- Competing priorities that sap time and energy
- Waning motivation
- Lowered self-confidence
- Additional knowledge, skills or techniques needed
- Their first choice career move not panning out.

Competing priorities often require discussion of some practical time management strategies, but sometimes they flag other issues like confidence. Waning motivation suggests a return to conversations about their values and why they chose this direction, but it might be a symptom of a fresh problem.

Address lack of confidence by reviewing strengths and past achievements. Perhaps your mentee has moved to a new role. If they feel a little uncertain — which is perfectly natural — your reassurance, as they gain experience over time will build their confidence. However, perhaps some conversations about specific issues that are challenging them are needed. Your problem-solving approach may help them develop strategies to use, and you may have opinions and suggestions from your own experience to offer. It may be that they need additional skills to grow into the new role, so help them find opportunities for development, through education, training or observing role models etc. Then assist them to set development goals and plans.

If they are not making headway on a goal that involves changing jobs, you need to establish where the problem is. Are they not finding jobs they can apply for? Are they applying, but not getting interviews/ Are they getting interviews, but not winning the job? Each of these shows a distinct problem, and each can be fixed.

Setbacks are usually temporary, and careers are a long-term project. A focus, not just on what's gone wrong, but what's gone well helps foster productive conversations about what they can do differently to overcome difficulties.

THERE IS **No Success Without Failure**

What if they cannot achieve the goal?

An older gentleman ran several successful businesses before his last one sent him broke. He and his wife had put their hearts and souls into the business, but they lost almost everything when the bank liquidated their assets. Just a few years later, he tells me it's the best thing that ever happened to him. They had a very tough first year after losing the business, but they took what they had, used their skills and experience and built a new and better life for themselves.

Failure that leads to a different sort of success is not an uncommon story.

You may have your own experience of something that was devastating at the time, but turned out to be the springboard for something much better. In fact, most people, successful in the arts, sports, business or science, will tell you that there is no success without failure. There are an abundance of examples. Look up Michael Jordan's missed shots and lost games. Steve Jobs, sacked from his own company! The Wright Brothers crashed many planes before the one that stayed in the air — for ten seconds.

Failure is disappointing and painful, but there is not a human on the planet who has not failed, we all do, often. Sometimes we don't notice. Sometimes we shrug our shoulders and get on with it, sometimes we give ourselves a really hard time, ruminating, blaming and locking ourselves into misery. Hopefully, we learn to pick ourselves up, dust ourselves off, and move on. We develop resilience when we use failure for learning.

Mindset is important and you will help your mentee most if you foster the following beliefs:

- You have failed; you are not a failure
- Setbacks are temporary
- Failure is feedback
- Blame is disempowering
- Failure is an opportunity to reset

You Have Failed; You Are Not a Failure.

Our society seems obsessed with success and few are taught how to cope with failure, let alone welcome it as an opportunity. An emotional response to failure is natural, and emotional pain can hurt as much as physical pain. Show your mentee empathy, listen as they express their feelings, but don't allow your mentee to label themselves as a failure. What they did didn't work, but it doesn't characterise who they are. Failure is an event, not a life sentence.

You will need to balance enabling them to sit with, or process, emotions and shifting their attention from the past and present to the future. If you rush them, they won't feel heard and you'll lose the trust and rapport you've built, but if you let them wallow, you risk them becoming stuck.

SETBACKS ARE **Temporary**

The pain of failure can seem all-encompassing, but it will pass. Listen to your mentee. Are they painting the event as catastrophic? Do they think this one failure will ruin their life, or destroy their future for ever? Help them put the failure into perspective. In the greater scheme of things, how much impact on them does this need to have? What other parts of their life will be completely unaffected? I don't want to use the platitude "what doesn't kill you makes you stronger", but it's sometimes true. Nothing lasts forever, circumstances do change, and people grow.

FAILURE IS **Feedback**

Failure means something was wrong. It's a chance to figure out what, so that you can rectify it. You can bet that the Wright Brothers (and all the other inventors trying to design aircraft) looked at each one of the crashed planes to figure out what went wrong and literally went back to the drawing board to try again.

The Dalai Lama said: "When you lose, don't lose the lesson". So help your mentee figure out what went wrong. Get them to reflect and get insight from the failure. There's usually more than one reason.

· · ·

BLAME IS DISEMPOWERING

Both blaming other people or circumstances, and blaming oneself are counter productive. Blame makes you a victim, helpless and powerless. Stephen Covey [2]writes about the circle of control — those things over which we have most influence and the circle of concern — those we care about, but cannot control (see chapter #). This is an extremely useful concept that will enable your mentee to take responsibility for what they did, or did not do, that contributed to failure and those factors they could do nothing about. You can then help them recognise missteps or mistakes, where they could have made better choices and what they will do differently in the future.

FAILURE IS an Opportunity to Reset

Sports people know the value of rest and recovery. After an immense effort, bodies must have rest to recover, brains do too. We can't work 24/7 without exhausting ourselves. We need recreation and relaxation to be effective. Goals, planning, achievement and failure are hard work. Your mentee may need a break for a while. Remind them of their work/life balance strategies and encourage them to take time out to refresh. Then they need to come back, roll up their sleeves and reset goals using what they've learned from the experience of failure. Don't linger too long once they've got the lessons. Rehashing the negative emotions, or poring over the "coulda, woulda, shouldas" is unhelpful.

This process has now equipped them to set new goals with realistic expectations and the benefit of hindsight.

HOW TO HANDLE Success

Hopefully, I've offered a realistic, practical and positive approach to failure. So let's end by talking about success. We encourage people to be humble about succeeding, but it is important to celebrate and take pride in the hard work of achievements. I have a few trusted friend with whom I share significant results — as soon as I finish, I'll be messaging a fellow author and mentor who will be as thrilled as I am that I completed my book!

As a mentor, you have created a safe space for your mentee to share their challenges and their triumphs. You can celebrate with them, congratulate and point out the measure of what they have achieved.

There are as many lessons to be learned from success as there are from failure. You can lead a conversation of reflection and review, a debriefing. The format is simple — what worked well, so you can repeat it in the future; what didn't work so well that you will avoid; and what would you do differently?

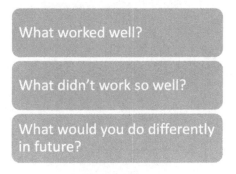

Figure 35: *Debrief*

One of the most wonderful things about mentoring is graciously accepting the gratitude of the mentee. You'll definitely point out that they were the ones that did the hard work, but hopefully it's been a pleasurable, rewarding and developmental process for you too.

The other beautiful thing is, most people who have been mentored often mentor others. Like the pebble tossed in the pool, the ripples spread out to the edges. Take joy from your contribution that will go far beyond what you may see or know.

PART IV

TOOLS AND GUIDES

This section contains guides, templates and activities for you to use with your mentee. You can provide printable copies to your mentee by downloading them here.

Insert https://dl.bookfunnel.com/anzljazhx3

I have used these materials with thousands of participants in my mentoring and career development workshops.

The activities draw out information that mentees need to make decisions. They can do these as "homework" between meetings. Most have suggested discussion questions that prepare the mentee for the reflective conversation you'll have after they complete the activity.

11

GUIDES

Quick Tips

- Create an appropriate environment
- Don't be in a rush, take time to get to know each other
- Establish expectations early
- Schedule meetings, meet regularly, have them confirm and add agenda items
- Re-establish rapport each time you speak
- Get them to commit to some actions, activity, research or reflection between every meeting
- Refer to specialists — a trained career coach, psychologist or counsellor when needed
- The career landscape changes. What was once true may no longer be the case
- You don't have all the answers — they must do their research
- Prepare for each conversation using the mentee's agenda
- Master good questions and the ability to draw them out
- Aim to have them talking 80% of the time
- Ask for and provide feedback on the process.

The Mentoring Code

Both mentor and mentee will:

Maintain the confidentiality of the content of their conversations, except in the case of disclosure of unlawful activities or threat of self-harm

Create an environment that enables both to focus on goals and professional development

Discuss each other's expectations of the relationship and how those expectations may be met

Recognise that the boundaries of mentoring are limited to professional and career-related goal achievement and that issues beyond this may require referral to another professional, such as a counsellor, therapist or specialist advisor

Appreciate that the mentor is not a professional consultant or intermediary and is not empowered to act on the mentee's behalf

Honour each other's time by managing accessibility and scheduling by mutual agreement

Fulfil their agreement to mentoring by staying in touch with their mentoring partner until the end of the program or an agreed relinquishment of the relationship

Understand that mentoring relationships exemplify dignity, autonomy and personal responsibility

Regularly review and provide feedback about their mentoring experience to each other

Ensure that they act with integrity and in such a way as to cause no harm to each other

Respect diversity and equity

Avoid exploitation of the relationship

Conduct themselves professionally and in a manner that reflects positively on the profession, the organisation and the mentoring program

Conclude the relationship respectfully when it ceases to be useful

A Mentoring Agreement

We commit to:

1. Regular Contact

Method(s): Can we get together in real-time, face-to-face, phone, or online (FaceTime/Skype/Zoom etc.) or, by email or online platform?

Term: Over what period of time do we intend the mentoring to take place?

Frequency: How often will we meet or be in touch?

Duration: How long will we meet for each time?

2. Professional Courtesy

Specific expectations (e.g. confirming appointments, preparing and agenda, being on time, etc.)

3. Ground Rules

What we will and won't do (e.g. Maintain confidentiality)

4. Scope and Boundaries

Topics we will/will not discuss

Signed (Mentor): Signed (Mentee):

DateDate

Pre-Meeting Checklist

Have you:

- Reviewed your agreed goals for mentoring?
- Agreed on the agenda or discussion topics for this meeting?
- Confirmed meeting time, duration and venue?
- Scheduled uninterrupted time for the meeting?
- Gathered any necessary information or resources?
- Prepared questions you want to ask?

Post-Meeting Checklist

Have you:

- Summarised what was discussed?
- Noted actions to be taken before next meeting?
- Obtained feedback about level of satisfaction with the mentoring process, communication style and progress toward outcomes?
- Agreed next meeting date?

First Meeting Agenda

You will create your own draft agenda for your first meeting, but it might include:

Confidentiality

Apart from any information shared that you are legally required or bound to report under your organisation's policies, it is usual to agree explicitly that the content of your conversations with the mentee is to be kept private. This works both ways, what the mentee discloses to you and anything you might share with them you do not want to go any further.

Purpose

You want to clarify the main reasons for the mentoring. Talk about desired outcomes/objectives, but recognise that these may unfold as the conversations progress. Your mentee may start with one aim in mind, but as you collaboratively explore, it may become apparent that something else is what they're after.

Expectations

Be clear about your ground-rules. Normal business etiquette should apply to both of you. Making and keeping appointments, confirming them, rescheduling only when absolutely unavoidable, and the mentee providing a dot-point agenda is standard.

You might also talk about having a review session to decide whether to continue or exit the mentoring after a few meetings, feedback so you know you're on track and not just letting the relationship fizzle out instead of fixing any difficulties.

Let them know that you're not a sponsor who will get them a job, or speak on their behalf and that they will do the work outside of your meetings.

Logistics & Contact

Discuss how often you'll meet (monthly is a minimum), the duration, and how — can you do face-to-face? Or will you do online meetings? Agree ways you'll communicate in between and confirm your meetings.

Other items

Some activities in this book could be completed by the mentee before you meet, especially Focus for Mentoring, and I recommend you swap a brief biography.

You'll probably want to talk about your backgrounds, work and life experiences, and some non-work interests you might have in common.

Ask the mentee to suggest additional agenda items and let them know they will prepare the agenda for future meetings. They can draft this towards the end of each meeting with your input. They then finalise it and send it to you with their meeting confirmation a day or so ahead of the meeting.

REVIEW MEETING WORKSHEET

The purpose of the review meeting is to improve the effectiveness of our mentoring and our enjoyment of the process. We will have a candid discussion and each provide honest feedback. Then we will either agree to continue mentoring together or, if we are having difficulties we feel we can't resolve, consider a no-fault opt out.

You can frame the conversation around the following questions, please reflect on them and prepare to share:

What has been achieved, so far, as a result of mentoring?

What is working well in our mentoring?

What's not working so well?

What are you enjoying/not enjoying in the mentoring?

What, done differently, could improve our mentoring?

What could each of us do differently or better?

Overall, how do you feel about our mentoring?

Do you want to continue?

Mentoring Evaluation

If you are in a structured mentoring program, there will be an evaluation process. If not, use these discussion starters to share feedback.

1. What did you each get out of the mentoring experience?
2. To what degree was good rapport established?
3. Were the mentee's needs addressed?
4. Did you achieve the goals nominated at the outset of the mentoring?
5. Were meetings of appropriate duration and frequency?
6. Has the mentee's ability to produce and sustain self-development improved as a result of mentoring?

7. How satisfied is the mentee with counsel and advice provided?
8. Was constructive and encouraging feedback provided when needed?
9. Was the mentee encouraged to accept responsibility for his or her own development?
10. What demonstrable outcomes can be attributed to the mentoring relationship?
11. How do you each feel about the mentoring?

12

TOOLS

This chapter contains 46 activities that I have used for many years, in career development and mentoring workshops for people employed in health, construction, energy, communications, education, law and government.

The aim of every activity is described, and the steps for completing it are included. Most have suggestions to guide your discussion afterwards.

Do not assign every activity to your mentee—they may get bored or slip into "analysis-paralysis! Simply choose the ones that seem most relevant. Download a printable copy here. https://dl.bookfunnel.com/anzljazhx3

Activity 1: Focus for Mentoring

Aim: *To clarify the focus for mentoring.*

1. *Tick the items below that best reflect your goals for your career conversations.*
2. *Select your top 3 priorities*
3. *Use this information to summarise your reasons for wanting to talk about your career right now.*

I want to:

- Explore choices, options, and possibilities for my future career
- Get more satisfaction from work
- Move into a new role in my organisation
- Move up or move into a leadership role
- Change my job/career
- Find work/life balance that's right for me
- Learn new skills and capabilities or obtain development opportunities
- Convince others of my capabilities
- Deal with challenges at work
- Other

Discussion:

What will be the main focus for your mentoring?

Activity 2: Your Career Path To Date

Aim: *To describe your career so far and identify what you liked and disliked about jobs, work or roles you've had*

1. *List each job or role you have had. Include voluntary positions, community service part-time and unpaid work.*
2. *Rate how satisfied you were with that job. Use a scale of 1-10, ten being most satisfying.*
3. *Summarise why you chose the job. What you liked/disliked most about it and why you left.*
4. *Reflect: What themes or patterns can you identify? What does this tell you about yourself?*

Job/Role	Rating	Liked	Disliked

Discussion:

What do you like/dislike in a role?

What satisfies you in your work?

Activity 3: Career Motivation

Aim: *To clarify and gain insight into some of your career motivations.*

In your career so far:

- What have you enjoyed most? What have you enjoyed least?
- What are your greatest skills? What are your poorest skills?
- List skills you'd most/least like to gain?
- Which areas interested you most? Which areas interested you least?
- Which tasks have motivated you most? Which tasks motivated you least?
- Which tasks have satisfied you most? Which tasks have satisfied you least?
- What types of people have motivated you most/least?
- What types of people have you got on well/poorly with?
- What level of responsibility do you feel comfortable handling?
- What working conditions suit you?
- Where do you want to live and work?
- What income level is important for you to attain?

Discussion:

What patterns do you see in the information?

Activity 4: Where Am I Now?

Aim: *To use art to tap into thoughts and feelings about work, life and career.*

1. *Draw a picture that represents you, your life and your work and how you feel about your career.*
2. *Reflect on the themes and insights highlighted by your drawing*

Discussion:

What are the key themes emerging for you?

Activity 5: Heroes Hall Of Fame

Aim: *To identify values and personal attributes to which you aspire.*

1. *Who are your heroes? List real people or fictional characters, well known or relatively unknown, living or no longer alive from any walk of life.*
2. *Pick one and state what you admire about them.*
3. *Note the values or characteristics that are significant for you*

The characteristics you describe give clues to your values, and attributes you may possess or aspire to.

Discussion:

What are the values and attributes demonstrated by the chosen heroes?

Activity 6: Three Dimensional Analysis

Aim: *To identify sources of satisfaction and dissatisfaction and things to look for in your future career.*

The concept of three-dimensional analysis was developed by Paul Stevens of Worklife, who suggested that for career choices that lead to success and fulfilment you need to analyse three dimensions:

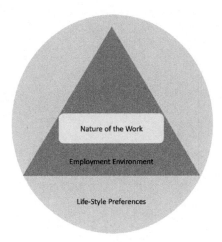

Nature of the Work: The tasks, activities and responsibilities of a job or occupation.

Employment Environment: An industry, profession, occupational field, type of organisation, workplace culture or style.

Life-Style Preferences: How you want to live your life. Issues of personal well being, family, and other important aspects of living.

1. *Rate on a scale of 10 (zero is low, 10 is high) the degree to which you are satisfied in each of the three dimensions.*
2. *List the aspects that satisfy or dissatisfy you.*
3. *List what you'd ideally want in each of the three dimensions.*

Discussion:

What does this mean in terms of what you want in future in your career?

Activity 7: Values Discovery

Aim: *To identify and prioritise values*

1. *Rate the following items 1 = Very important, 2 = Moderately important, or 3 = Not important*

Achievement: desired outcomes resulting from persistent endeavour

1 2 3

Aesthetics: appreciation and enjoyment of beauty and artistic experiences

1 2 3

Altruism: active concern for the needs and values of others

1 2 3

Ancestry: those who came before us; our line of descent

1 2 3

Autonomy: the drive to be an independent, self-determining individual

1 2 3

Community: people who care about something and pursue it together

1 2 3

Competency/Skill: competence in performing given tasks

1 2 3

Control/Influence: authority or influence over others

1 2 3

Creativity: the ability to transcend traditional ideas, rules, patterns, relationships, or the like to create meaningful new ideas, forms, methods and interpretations

1 2 3

Dignity: demonstrate behaviour and stature that earn the respect of self and others

1 2 3

Emotional Well-being: inner peace, abiding confidence, freedom from anxieties, tranquility

1 2 3

Family: person(s) with whom you have an emotional and/or biological bond

1 2 3

Harmony: unity in relationships; the absence of conflict and strife between associates

1 2 3

Health: soundness of body, mind and spirit

1 2 3

Honesty: truth, openness, fairness, integrity

1 2 3

Honour: a recognition bestowed on one who has distinguished him/herself from peers by living a life of superior standing

1 2 3

Humility: the ability to be honest with yourself, meek, teachable, open to change

1 2 3

Justice: Behaviour that conforms to what is right, fair and reasonable

1 2 3

Knowledge: fact and lessons learned, understanding/awareness of principles that organise and explain

1 2 3

Love: unselfish devotion that freely accepts another person

1 2 3

Loyalty: maintained allegiance to a person, group, institution or idea

1 2 3

Passion: the "fire within" that brings rewards beyond any monetary gain or satisfaction from your hard work

1 2 3

Personal Growth: Lifelong learning, continuous improvement, wisdom

1 2 3

Physical Appearance: concern for the attractiveness of one's own body

1 2 3

Pleasure: enjoyment and gratification delivered from that which is to one's liking

1 2 3

Recognition: favourable attention and acknowledgement from others that makes one feel significant

1 2 3

Relationships: being surrounded by people who like you and care about you

1 2 3

Spirituality/Religion: a set of beliefs concerning the cause, nature, and purpose of the universe. Communion with, and activity in a relationship with a higher power

1 2 3

Wealth: an abundance of valued material possessions and resources. Economic prosperity

1 2 3

2. Highlight your top 7 from the above list.

3. Number your top 3 in priority order.

Discussion:

How do these values play out in your life and/or career?

Activity 8: Meeting Your Values

Aim: *To consider ways to meet career values.*

1. *List values that are not currently met in your job.*
2. *Describe ways that your values could be met.*

Discussion:

Are there ways that these could be incorporated into your current job?

What kinds of occupations might meet your values?

Activity 9: Achievements

Aim: *Self-appreciation, to identify talents and potential strengths and to prepare information that could be used in job interviews.*

1. *The line below represents the years of your life until now, divide it into four periods. List your achievements in each period.*

The achievements you list could relate to work; home; personal family; sporting; education; community; hobbies; leisure etc. They should be events of significance to you. Don't discount ideas by saying "oh that wasn't important". If it meant something to you, you were satisfied and proud of achieving it, it belongs on your list!

0_____Present

Age 0 to ....

Age .... to ....

Age .... to ....

Age .... to Present

2. *Pick two or three of your most satisfying achievements to describe in more detail.*

3. *What did you do?*

4. *How, specifically, did you do you it?*

5. *What were the results?*

Discussion:

What themes or patterns can you identify?

What talents or strengths were evident in these achievements?

Are these talents or strengths used in the mentee's current role?

How could they be used in a future role?

Activity 10: Strengths Discovery

Aim: *To identify talents and potential strengths.*

The best way to discover talents is with an objective assessment. I recommend the CliftonStrengths Assessment available online here: https://www.gallupstrengthscenter.com

Consider writing a reflective journal. It will take some time, but can be extremely rewarding to write introspectively, putting your thoughts and feelings on paper.

Here are some thought-starter questions you could reflect on:

- What do you look forward to doing most at work?
- Which activities do you complete quickly and easily?
- What do you enjoy doing most outside of work?
- What did you enjoy doing most in previous roles?
- What do other people say you do best?
- What are you known for?
- What is your dream job? Why?
- After living expenses, what do you spend your money on?
- What did you love as a child?
- What would friends and co-workers say were your talents?

Discussion

What clues to talents and strengths can you pick up from the answers to the questions above?

In terms of personality, do the answers reveal more of a doer, persuader, people-person or someone who loves information?

Activity 11: Strengths Thirty-Day Challenge

Aim: *To identify talents and potential strengths.*

1. *Every day, at least once a day, stop and reflect: What did I do well? Write it down - especially if you enjoyed it, especially if you felt strong when you did it!*
2. *At the end of thirty days, share with your mentor. Look for patterns and evidence of your talent themes and strengths.*

Discussion:

What themes and patterns emerge?

What clues to talents and strengths can you pick up?

Do these cause point to a doer, persuader, people-person or someone who loves information?

Activity 12: Write a Personal Mission Statement

Aim: *To create an over-arching aim for your life.*

Organisations use mission statements to express their reason for being. A mission statement gives purpose, direction and meaning to day-to-day activities. You can benefit by developing personal mission statements. It can help you:

- Reduce stress due to conflicting desires
- Focus your energy and efforts
- Set meaningful goals which will bring satisfaction
- Clarify your priorities
- Create work and life balance
- Maintain personal integrity; and,
- Provide a whole-of-life perspective

1. *Read the mission statement of your organisation and others to get a feel for the characteristics of a mission statement*
2. *View Tools for Mentoring Video 3 Personal Strategic Planning*
3. *Search online for examples of personal mission statements from well-known people such as Oprah Winfrey, Richard Branson, Malala Yousafzai, etc.*
4. *Draft brief statements about who you would like to be, what you would like to do and what your strengths are*
5. *Review and revise. Look for common themes*
6. *A single word, phrase, or theme may emerge that resonates with you. Adopt this. See how it feels.*

Discussion:

What themes or patterns can you identify?

Do these represent your highest self?

Could you sum up in a motto of just a few words?

Activity 13: Skills Audit

Aim: *To identify the many skills you currently have. To increase your ability to find roles for which you can match requirements.*

1. *Use the Functional Skills and Personal Attributes checklists (on following pages) to identify skills you possess. List them.*
2. *Review your job description and list skills mentioned and implied*
3. *Refer to your performance appraisal and list skills that appear there*
4. *Add skills you've used in previous jobs*
5. *Include skills gained through education and training*
6. *List skills developed through life experience, tasks, hobbies, sport, and activities outside of work*
7. *Add skills obtained through community involvement, church, club or voluntary activities*
8. *Include skills learned through family responsibilities*
9. *List any other areas of knowledge, skills, natural talents, or abilities you have*
10. *Ask people who know you to describe 3 of your personal attributes*

Discussion:

What themes or patterns can you identify?

Which skills are you best at?

Which do you enjoy most?

Which skills fall into both "best at" and "enjoy most"?

Do you use these in your current work?

Activity 14: Functional Skills Checklist

Aim: *To expand the list of skills in your skills audit.*

1. *Highlight items on the Functional Skills Checklist (next page) That you are good at and enjoy doing.*

achieving	developing	organising
adapting	diagnosing	organising
addressing	directing	persuading
administering	editing	planning
advising	estimating	preparing
analysing	evaluating	presenting
arranging	explaining	problem solving
assessing	formulating	producing
auditing	gathering	promoting
budgeting	identifying	publicising
building	implementing	publishing
calculating	improvising	purchasing
checking	initiating	questioning
classifying	innovating	quoting
coaching	integrating	recruiting
compiling	investigating	reporting
controlling	leading	representing
coordinating	mediating	styling
counselling	modelling	supervising
creating	monitoring	systemizing
deciding	negotiating	testing
defining	observing	training
designing	operating	writing

Activity 15: Personal Skills Checklist

Aim: *To expand the list of skills in your skills audit.*

1. *Highlight the Personal Attributes (next page) That you are good at and enjoy doing.*

analytical	efficient	practical
aloof	frank	precise
agreeable	friendly generous	rational
artistic adventurous	gregarious	reserved
aggressive	helpful	radical
benevolent cautious	hard-headed happy	rebellious
critical complicated	intellectual	receptive
creative	independent	responsible
capable	introspective	shrewd
curious	idealistic	sociable
confident	imaginative	speculative
content conforming	impulsive intuitive	striving
conscientious	kind	self-controlled
conservative	methodical	stable
conventional	materialistic	sincere
dreamy	natural	sensitive scholarly
dominant	nonconforming	scientific
dogmatic	persuasive	tactful
energetic	persistent	trusting thorough
enterprising	Popular	thrifty
enthusiastic	power-seeking	understanding
extroverted	pleasure-seeking	versatile
		witty
		warm

Activity 16: Turn Personal Attributes into Skills

Aim: *To expand the list of skills in your skills audit*

1. *List skills associated with the following personal characteristics:*

Patience = the ability to

Friendly = the ability to

Confident = the ability to

Methodical = the ability to

Helpful = the ability to

2. *Take each of the personal attributes you chose in the previous activity and apply the same process as above.*

3. *Add these to your skills audit list*

Activity 17: Transferrable Skills

Aim: *To expand the list of skills in your skills audit.*

Few people have ever identified the full range of skills they possess. Most people accumulate skills throughout their lifetime and many skills are transferable, they can be used in a variety of roles. For example, skills associated with organising an appointment schedule are equally useful to a secretary, a sales representative or a plumber.

All your people skills are transferable because communicating and dealing with people is the same in a motor registry, a hospital or building site. Many technical skills are transferable, and even knowledge and skills that seem unique to a particular may have transferable components.

1. *Review your skills audit and highlight those that are transferrable.*

Activity 18: Motivated Skills

Aims: *To identify the skills most likely to bring you satisfaction and success in your career. To choose skills to focus on when you are researching possibilities.*

It is very beneficial for you to identify your motivated skills and prioritise these when researching your options. Motivated skills are those that you are good at and enjoy doing.

1. *List work and non-work activities and accomplishments that you did well, are proud of, or enjoy most.*
2. *Describe what you did and how you did it*
3. *Distil from these descriptions the skills that you used*
4. *Include these in your skills audit*
5. *Review your skills audit and highlight those you'd classify as your motivated skills.*

Activity 19: Analyse Your Capabilities

Aim: *To identify capabilities you have and those you could develop. To increase your awareness of options. To express your knowledge, skills and abilities in the language recruiters use.*

Capabilities include knowledge and abilities as well as skills necessary for various roles.

1. *If your organisation has a capability framework (or similar) and you can access it, do. If not, find The Capability Framework (NSW) or the equivalent in your location online and download it.*
2. *Read the document to get a feel for it.*
3. *Compare your job/role description to the framework and identify capabilities that match or are very similar.*
4. *Compare the lists from your Skills Audit and the other skills activities and identify capabilities that match or are very similar.*

Discussion:

Are there themes or patterns that suggest talents and strengths?

Are there areas you'd like to develop?

Does this analysis point to occupations or roles that would allow you to use your strengths?

Activity 20: Career Portfolio Checklist

Aims: *To collate easily accessible information that you can use in job applications, one your resumé and in interviews.*

A career portfolio might be a ring binder with plastic sleeves, a file-box with a series of folders or a folder with files on your computer. Whatever format suits you, this portfolio contains all relevant information about your career.

1. Prepare, collect and organise the following items:

- Your career goals
- List of competences
- List of achievements
- Resumés and/or curriculum vitae
- Certificates, diplomas, degrees, awards
- Job descriptions
- Performance appraisals
- References or letters of recommendation or compliments
- Record of training, development and education
- Samples of your work
- List of your previous supervisors
- Referees with their current contact details
- Any other relevant documentation

Activity 21: Areas for Development

Aim: *To identify areas for further development*

1. *Skills or attributes that would enhance my current performance include:*
2. *Skills or attributes that I may need to develop for the future are:*
3. *Capabilities I'd like to take up to the next level are:*
4. *Further training, development or education that may be of value to me includes:*
5. *Other areas I'd like to develop are:*

Discussion:

Which areas will you prioritise for development?

How might you develop in these areas?

Activity 22: Deal With Your Inner Critic

Aim: *To reduce the impact of negative self-talk and find more constructive thoughts.*

We all have an inner critic. If it is uncontrolled, it will deliver a stream of negative self-talk that reinforces limiting beliefs, undermines confidence and keeps us fearful. So, it's worth recognising and managing the messages rather than allowing them to influence us unchecked. Here are some ways to do that:

1. *Tune into the voice of the inner critic and what it says. Ask yourself, would you criticise anyone else so harshly? Would you let anyone else speak to you that way, unchallenged?*
2. *Use rational thinking to come up with evidence to the contrary.*
3. *If you think the criticism holds some truth, how would a good friend more kindly give you this feedback?*
4. *Notice the inner critic speaking. Label it or give it a name and imagine it as a slightly ridiculous cartoon character, doing a silly walk. Have a phrase you say as it starts up, like: "Here is the inner critic again, doing what it does."*
5. *Practice compassion. The inner critic judges you and other people. When you find yourself judging others, remind yourself that you don't have all the facts. Give people the benefit of the doubt. Be kindly in your thoughts toward others. It is then easier to be self-compassionate, kind to yourself.*
6. *Learn to modify self-talk. Consider alternatives below.*

Modify Self-Talk	
I always ...	Sometimes I ... but now I'll ...
I'll never ...	I haven't tried ... yet
I can't ...	I don't know if I can ... yet
I must ...	I might ...
I should ...	I could ...
Everyone knows ...	Some people might think ...
It's awful	It's inconvenient/upsetting
That would be terrible	That's not my preferred outcome

Activity 23: Self-Critique to Self-Improvement

Aim: *To discover ways to use self-critique for improvement.*

An inner critic isn't all bad! You need to know when you mess up so that you can improve. Just don't beat yourself up about shortcomings.

Here's how to self-critique constructively so that you can learn from either a positive or negative outcome:

1. *Describe the situation or task*
2. *Detail what did you do or not do that led to the outcome. Leave out any judgement, simply state objectively what you did.*
3. *List what went well, that you'd do again in future*
4. *List what did not go well that you wouldn't repeat*
5. *Brainstorm some ideas for things you could do as well or instead of those you've listed. If you're not sure, ask a trusted friend, colleague or mentor for input.*
6. *Create some general principles to guide your actions in similar circumstances in future*
7. *Review and remind yourself of these principles regularly and act on them*

Activity 24: Update Beliefs About Yourself

Aim: *To develop constructive beliefs that serve and support career satisfaction.*

Negative beliefs can become self-fulfilling prophesies. In other words, what you believe causes you to behave in ways that conform to the belief.

Often, negative beliefs are accumulated over time. A bit like a computer system, operating in the background, influencing how things are done. Like a computer system you need to update beliefs, or they won't serve you as well as they could.

1. *List three negative beliefs that do not serve you.*
2. *Rewrite them in a more constructive way (see examples below). Think of yourself as a spin-doctor, preparing a bio that shows someone in their best light.*
3. *Train yourself to notice when you tell yourself anything that implies you are "too" anything or not something "enough". Replace these thoughts with a constructive alternative.*

Update Beliefs	
I'm too old/young	It might be a challenge for someone my age, but others have, and I can too
I'm not smart enough	I'd need to develop the knowledge and skills for that
I'm a failure	I had a go, and it didn't work out, but here's what I learned
I'm no good at ...	It will be a steep learning curve
I can't ...	I haven't yet

Activity 25: Seven Career Directions

Aims: *To consider a variety of career moves.*

1. *Identify examples of each of the following career moves.*
2. *List the advantages and disadvantages of each move.*

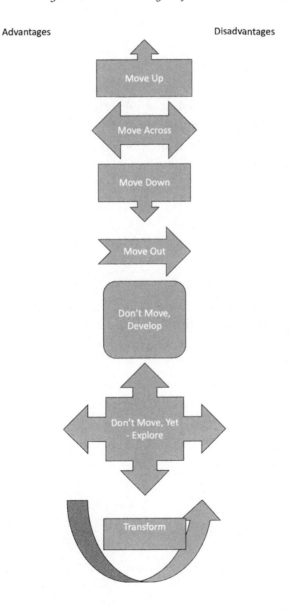

Activity 26: Moving Up Checklist

Aims: *To consider the viability of seeking a higher-level position in my organisation.*

Moving up in an organisation the traditional way people have progressed in the past, but it is not automatic. It depends upon you developing and enhancing your capabilities, being in an organisation that has such opportunities and being able to compete successfully against other applicants.

1. *What the current and future skills in demand in your industry/field/organisation?*
2. *Do you have them, or are you in the process of developing them?*
3. *Are there positions available one or two levels above yours?*
4. *What are the knowledge, skills, attributes and experience listed in the role descriptions?*
5. *Do you meet these criteria?*
6. *Have you demonstrated high-level performance in your current job?*
7. *Have you taken on projects, served on a task force or contributed in some way that would support your case for promotion?*
8. *Have you the experience necessary for a more senior role?*
9. *Do you have a positive image/profile/reputation within your organisation?*
10. *Have you published, presented or taken part in industry associations, professional bodies or community groups?*
11. *Have you gained leadership experience or qualifications?*
12. *What evidence can you provide of your capability?*
13. *Is your resumé ready?*

Discussion:

Is moving up a possibility to consider?

Activity 27: Lateral Move Checklist

Aims: *To explore moves that would not bring higher status or pay, but could offer opportunities to grow, broaden experience, or increase satisfaction.*

You may choose to gain broader experience by moving across to take a role that does not change your status or pay.

This could make them you competitive for a future upward move, expose you to a new leader, different people and work, allow you to develop or expand skills, and/or refresh your interest and enthusiasm.

1. *What other areas of your organisation interest you?*
2. *How could you learn more about these areas?*
3. *What the current and future skills in demand in these areas?*
4. *Do I have them, or am I developing them?*
5. *Are there roles available or likely to be available soon?*
6. *What are the knowledge, skills, attributes and experience listed in the role descriptions?*
7. *What transferrable skills would fit with these roles?*
8. *What evidence can I provide of my capability?*
9. *Have I demonstrated high-level performance in my current job?*
10. *Do I have a positive image/profile/reputation within my organisation?*

Discussion:

Is a lateral move a possibility to consider?

Activity 28: Moving Down Checklist

Aims: *To contemplate a temporary move to a lower-level position for work-life balance at a crucial time, or to learn new capabilities that equip me for a future new career direction.*

1. *It is sometimes worth moving down to learn and grow in a different area, perhaps to launch a new career or profession, or for work-life balance. There are a growing number of parents unwilling to forgo important life events for the demands of their job, and it's not just women who feel the pressure of balancing parenthood and work.*
2. *What are your reasons for this move?*
3. *Can you articulate your reasons clearly, concisely and positively?*
4. *What personal adjustments will you make to get the most from this role?*
5. *What are the financial implications of this move and how will you deal with them?*
6. *If for work-life balance, what steps can you take to ensure you can move back up again, if you want to, when personal demands ease?*
7. *If for development, how will you gain and track the learning you seek?*
8. *How will you ensure that you develop appropriate relationships with your new peer group and manager?*
9. *What will you do to show high commitment and performance in this role?*

Discussion:

Is moving down a possibility to consider?

Activity 29: Moving Out Checklist

Aims: *To make an informed decision about leaving the organisation and ensure an amicable parting.*

If there are no suitable opportunities, the culture is unsupportive or there is a lack of alignment of values, it may be necessary to move out of the organisation.

Better pay and status, a shorter commute or a myriad of other benefits may be attractive. However, people should do their homework and make informed decisions before leaving one organisation for another, to avoid disappointment.

1. *What are your reasons for this move?*
2. *Have you thoroughly researched the new organisation, its culture, management style and opportunities?*
3. *What are the advantages and disadvantage of this move?*
4. *Are you leaving on good terms with your manager, co-workers and the organisation?*
5. *What have you done to prepare for your new role?*

Discussion:

Is moving out a possibility to consider?

Activity 30: Don't Move - Develop

Aim: *To explore the scope for development within your current role. To determine whether this could be the right move for you.*

It is possible to overlook possibilities for increasing satisfaction within a current role. There may be ways to grow, develop capabilities, do more of what you love or include more interesting.This is known as job enrichment. It may take some creativity to find ways you can use the strengths and motivated skills and, it will require the cooperation and collaboration of your manager and team-members. However, good leaders will encourage this. It may also be a short-term solution.

1. *What aspects your role do you love?*
2. *How could you get more of that every day?*
3. *How might you be better at your job?*
4. *How does this role connect to your purpose/values/personal goals?*
5. *What would make this role more interesting/satisfying for you?*
6. *What the current and future skills in demand in your field?*
7. *What can you do do acquire capabilities for the future?*
8. *Have you had a conversation with your manager about job enrichment?*
9. *Are there tasks you could swap with co-workers to enrich both your jobs?*
10. *Are there projects or tasks forces you could contribute to?*
11. *How will you ensure that job enrichment doesn't become job enlargement – that is you just take on more work on top your existing role?*

Discussion:

Is developing within your current role a possibility to consider?

Activity 31: Don't Move Yet—Explore

Aims: *To continue to research and/or prepare for your next career move.*

A short-term strategy might be don't move, yet - explore. It may be necessary to continue to investigate possible career moves, or the chosen direction may need further planning, education or skills development. Some people take on a side-hustle, something they do free-lance or part-time as well as their day job, either to test the water, build up to a viable business or simply for the love of what they do out of hours.

1. *How will you maintain motivation and performance while you do your research or preparation?*
2. *Do you have a personal professional development plan?*
3. *Can you safely discuss your desires and intentions with your manager?*

Discussion:

What are your next steps?

Activity 32: Career Transformation

Aim: *To prepare for a complete change of career.*

Another option is to partially or totally transform your career. This might involve re-skilling, developing a different skill-set, a new career path through formal education, or starting your own business.

Business start-up is a very specialised area, there will be financial issues, local laws, health and safety, compliance and tax issues to master. Business start-up probably requires a mentor with expertise in both entrepreneurship and business management.

1. *Are you satisfied that you have all the data to make an informed decision to make this move?*
2. *What are the advantages and disadvantages of this move?*
3. *What re-skilling, new skill-sets, experience or qualifications will be required?*
4. *How will you gain these?*
5. *Do you have the resources you need for this transition?*
6. *Do you have support from others for this transition?*
7. *What else do you need to do to prepare?*
8. *How long is the transition likely to take?*

Discussion:

What are your next steps?

Activity 33: Options Exploration

Aim: *to identify potential career moves and begin to evaluate them*

Use the thought starters below to explore **seven** career moves described previously.

Note: A career move may not fit one description, it could be a combination of two or more e.g. vertical and relocation or lateral and enrichment. You should thoroughly explore *several* different moves that are attractive to you - even if the possibility of making the move seems remote at this time. Also explore one or two moves that seem less attractive to you at this time. The purpose of this exercise is to gain further insight into your career decision-making process as well as lay a foundation for you career goal setting and planning.

1. *A move I want to explore is:*
2. *The advantages and disadvantages of this move are:*
3. *This move satisfies/contradicts my career values in the following ways:*
4. *The transferable skills, knowledge credentials and experience that support this move are:*
5. *Additional skills, knowledge credentials and experience that I may need to make this move are:*
6. *Perceived constraints and personal choices that may prevent me making this move are:*
7. *Barriers (within or outside the organisation) that may be obstacles if I make this move are:*
8. *Other factors that I need to consider before deciding whether this move is a career goal for me at this time are:*
9. *Additional research I need to do before deciding whether this move is a career goal for me at this time are:*
10. *Additional decision criteria I will use to evaluate this move are:*
11. *In terms of matching my desired job content, employment environment and lifestyle preferences, I rate this move:*

Discussion:

What are your next steps?

Activity 34: Career Aim

Aim: *To ensure that career decisions include not only the nature of the work, but the work environment and lifestyle considerations as well.*

1. *Review your Three-Dimensional Analysis, values, skills and strengths activities*
2. *Draft an overall career goal using the formula below:*

I'd like a role that allows me to use my strengths and capabilities such as... Where the nature of the work involves... The work environment is... And that meets my highest priority lifestyle preferences of...

Discussion:

What occupations or roles might fulfil this career aim?

Activity 35: Dartboard

Aim: *To identify potential areas in which to set goals, useful topics of conversation and life balance issues.*

1. *Take a large (A3) piece of paper. Draw the largest circle you can fit on it. Now draw a second and third concentric circle within the first.*
2. *Divide the circle into about 12 segments by drawing straight lines and put a "bullseye" in the centre so the diagram resembles a dartboard.*

3. Brainstorm a list of the important areas of your life for which you need goals eg. relationship, family, career, health, money, spirituality, professional development, social contribution, fun, friends, hobbies, home, sport etc. Use these to label each segment in the outer ring.

4. Working on one segment of the dartboard, one important area at a time, write in the next ring, a brief description of how that aspect of your life is now.

5. When you have completed how it is now, move to the inner circle of each segment and describe, ideally, how you would like that part of your life to be.

6. Wherever you have a difference between how it is and how you'd like it to be, you have scope to set goals. These are not yet goals, but they are the foundation of your goal setting.

In the bull's eye, write the letter "I" to remind you that you are at the centre of your circle of influence. You have most control over your own thoughts, feelings, words and deeds. The "I" also stands for integrity, being true to your highest values and drawing together all the important parts of your life, rather than allowing them to pull you in different directions.

Activity 36: The Clock

Aim: *To gain insight and motivation as a basis for goal setting.*

1. Take a sheet of paper and draw a large circle. Create a clock face by writing "12", "3", "6" and "9" in the appropriate spots. Draw the "big hand" of your clock, pointing to 12. Above the "12" put zero.

2. Consider the next question quickly—your intuition will provide an answer and you can always change your mind later. Here is the question: To what age do you expect to live? Write this number to the left of the zero.

3. Now, using the zero and the number you just wrote as your life expectancy, draw the "little hand" on the clock face according to your present age. For example, if you said you'd live to 100 and you are now 50, the little hand points to 6 o'clock.

4. You have divided your circle into two parts, past and future. Your next task is to list your significant achievements to date. Record accomplishments of which you are proud, things you're glad you've done, experiences you've had and times you have been exactly who you want to be. Don't get hung up on words like "achievement" or "accomplishment". Whatever matters to you, matters.

5. Next, list the things you'd not want to leave undone when you go. Whether it's learning to sing, travel, reconciling old differences, reuniting with loved ones, material accoutrements, providing for others, or simply satisfying yourself. Write from the heart, describe your desires, list what matters to you.

6. You may wish to sort this list into ideas for the next five years, the five after that and the five after that. You will also break your first five years into lists for each year once you have decided which of these to make goals for action and which to leave on a wish list.

7. Most people like to spend the last part of life relaxing, smelling the roses or otherwise enjoying the fruits of life's labour. So, draw another line, at the point of your choice, to show your age of retirement on the clock. You can now calculate the number of

years left to achieve the financial security you'll need then. You also have a time frame for travel plans or experiences for which youth and strength are helpful. Identify other important points on the clock. If you have children, at what age will they no longer be dependent? Are there other age-related goals or changes?

Activity 37: Life Goals

Aim: *To ensure career choices fit with personal goals*

Human beings are by nature goal oriented. Clarifying goals will help you achieve what you want in life and add focus to your career goals.

You cannot manage work-life balance without priorities and life goals will help you set priorities.

1. *What are the things you want to do in your lifetime?*
2. *What are your personal goals for the next 10-20 years?*
3. *What are your goals for the next 2-5 years?*
4. *What do you want to achieve in the next 6 months?*
5. *What must you action in the next 3 months?*
6. *What will you do in the next 30 days?*
7. *What is your first step?*

Discussion:

What are the long and shorter-term life goals you'll work on?

Will these be included in the mentoring?

Activity 38: Priority Checklist

Aim: *To ensure that a career decision meets your highest priorities.*

1. *Review your Career Aim*
2. *State the decision you are evaluating, i.e. "accept job offer x"*
3. *Check off the items below:*

Decision:

- *I have researched this course of action*
- *This choice fits my interests, preferences, values*
- *It is a good match for my strengths and capabilities*
- *It's a move that will advance my short/long-term aspirations*
- *It's an opportunity to test/explore a career path*
- *This option could open new possibilities*
- *I believe this would be very satisfying*
- *I have the resources I need to pursue this option*

Discussion:

Are you ready to decide, or do you need to bounce around ideas some more?

What support will you need to make/ implement your decision?

Activity 39: Decision-Making Criteria

Aim: *To summarise interests, preferences, values and priorities to take into account when deciding*

We frequently hear people say: "this ticks all my boxes", decision-making criteria are simply what's in those boxes for choosing one career direction over another.

Having clear criteria–factors upon which your decision depends–makes choosing much easier.

1. *Review your previous activities and list what you'll take into account when considering options*
2. *Divide your list into Must Haves, Want to Haves, Nice to Have. (You might colour code your list with highlighters). Then rank the Must Haves in order of importance.*
3. *Are there any deal-breakers, things you will not do without?*
4. *Weigh each of your options against your criteria, but remember, it's not strictly a numbers game, there's room for gut feeling.*

Discussion:

Which is your first preference (Plan A)?

What's your second choice (Plan B)?

Activity 40: Force-field Analysis

Aim: *To identify practical actions to move you toward to your goal.*

Flip charts or whiteboards are good to use, but large sheets of paper will do just as well.

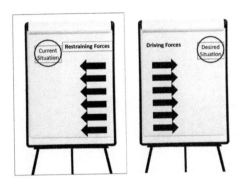

1. *Discuss and succinctly define the outcome you want to improve. Write this as the desired situation–where you want to be.*
2. *Discuss and briefly describe the current situation–where you are now. List this on another sheet, place to the left of the first.*
3. *Brainstorm a list of restraining forces -factors that hinder or work against you in achieving the desired outcome.*
4. *Brainstorm a list of driving forces things that help or would increase your ability to accomplish the desired outcome.*
5. *You can illustrate the strength of each of the forces working for and against you, by applying an impact rating of 1-5 (5 is strongest) and drawing an arrow toward or away from the outcome of a corresponding length and make the thickness of the arrow represent its relative importance.*
6. *Then brainstorm actions that could increase each driving force and decrease the impact of each restraining force.*
7. *Sort out the most practical and easiest to implement and create an action plan.*

Discussion:

What is your first step?

Activity 41: Career Control

Aim: *Empowerment by recognising which aspects of your career are, and are not, within your control, so you can focus your energy and efforts where they will do most good.*

In any situation, there are things you can control and things you can't. In the illustration below, the centre circle represents that which is within your power to influence. The outer circle represents aspects of the situation that may concern you but over which you have little control.

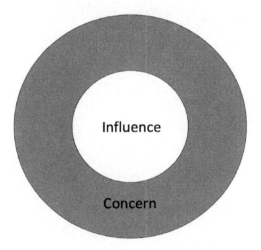

Source: Inspired by Covey, S. (1989) The Seven Habits of Highly Effective People. The Business Library

In any situation, what a person has most influence over, the epicentre of their circle of control, is themself. You have control over what you do, what you say and what you think.

1. *List aspects of your career over which you have most influence*
2. *List aspects of your career that concern you but over which you have less influence.*

Discussion:

What have you learned from this activity?

How will you use this insight?

Activity 42: Risk Management

Aim: *To identify and manage risks associated with particular career moves*

Consider the costs, personally, financially, socially and psychologically, as well as unintended or potentially negative consequences. For example, further studies will cost you time and money, there could be implications for your personal relationships, or trade-offs between this and other life goals. A shift to another role or organisation may not work out for any number of reasons. What would that mean for you? A downward move may bring loss of status and lower pay. How will that affect you?

1. *Brainstorm a list of potential negative or unintended consequences that could occur*
2. *List some things you could do to prevent each of these consequences*
3. *In case you can't prevent them, note what you could do to reduce the negative impact*
4. *If your actions to prevent and minimise these risks fail, what will you do to best manage the situation?*

Discussion:

How do you feel about the risks and your risk-management strategies?

Activity 43: Plan A B & Z

Aim: *To create back-up plans if your first choice doesn't work out.*

Plan A is your first choice of career direction, and you have a second choice, plan B.

1. MY "PLAN A"

2. MY "PLAN B" if this doesn't work out

3. MY "PLAN Z" for a worst-case scenario

Activity 44: Goal Analysis

Aim: *To clarify your goal and begin to plan how to achieve it.*

Sometimes we experience difficulties achieving goals. It may be because other priorities distract us, conflicting desires, or just not knowing where to start. Take some time to analyse why you want this goal, what you need to do, how you'll go about it, what resources you'll need and what else may occur or be possible as a result of your efforts.

Why?

For what purpose do you want to achieve this goal? Is it an end in itself or the means to an end? If it is a means to an end, what other means to this end have you considered?

What?

What, specifically, do you need to do? Are these separate goals requiring action plans of their own?

How?

List action steps necessary. Are there obstacles to be overcome? If so, how will you deal with them? What resources will you need? How will you get them?

What Else?

What may be possible for you as a result of the actions you take? Are there undesirable outcomes that may occur? If so, how will you deal with them?

Activity 45: Know Your Outcomes

Aim: *To create an awareness of the value of an outcome approach.*

Moving through your day without a desired outcome is like travelling without a destination. You may end up in a place you really want to be, or not. Enjoying the journey is a good outcome if it what you're aiming for, but not getting to your chosen destination may be have consequences you don't like.

Any action, or inaction, produces outcomes. Awareness of your most important outcomes helps keep you on track.

1. Practice outcome thinking:

Compiling your "to do" list for the day

- think: what outcomes do I want?

Preparing for a meeting:

think: what outcomes do I want?

In an argument with someone you care about, stop

think: what outcomes do I want?

Planning a social occasion

think: what outcomes do I want?

Preparing a meal

think: what outcomes do I want?

Working on your budget

think: what outcomes do I want?

2. Now, start drafting the outcomes that will enable you to achieve your career aim.

DISCUSSION:

What are the career outcomes you seek

Activity 46: Action Plan

Aim: *To document the details of your plan*

An action plan gets on paper the specific details of how you will achieve your goal. Use the information produced by your Goal Analysis and consolidate this information using a template like the one below, so that you document:

Aim: Purpose, intent, reason why you want this goal

Outcome: Tangible, measurable result you are aiming for

Actions: What you will do, how you will do it (list steps in sequential order)

Resources: Information, support, new skills, time, money, assistance from other people needed

Time Frame: When you will start, when you plan to finish and dates for the accomplishment of each step.

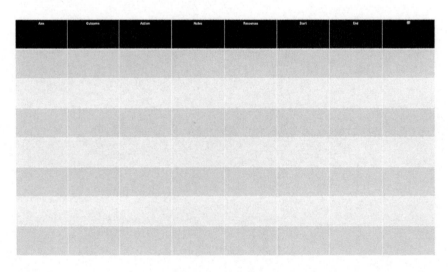

Aim	Outcome	Action	Notes	Resources	Start	End	●

ONLINE VIDEO MODULES

Tools for Mentoring is a self-paced career-planning course is made up of nine short (10-15 minute) videos and worksheets that you or your mentee can access anytime here:

http://mentoring-works.com/tools-for-mentoring/

Use the Password AMTCC21

∿

RECCOMMENDED READING

Marcus **Buckingham** and Donald **Clifton** (2001) *Now Discover Your Strengths*. The Free Press.

Michael Bungay-Stanier (2020) *The Advice Trap* Box of Crayons Press

Stephen **Covey** (1989) *The Seven Habits of Highly Effective People*. The Business Library

Barbara Fredrickson (2010) *Positivity*. Three Rivers Press

Heidi Grant-Halvorson (2012) *9 Things Successful People Do Differently*. Harvard Business Review Press

Beverly **Kaye**, Lindy **Williams**, Lynn **Coward** (2017) *Up is not the Only Way - Rethinking Career Mobility*. Career Systems International

Daniel **Pink** (2009) *Drive, The Surprising Truth About What Motivates Us*. Riverhead Books

Martin Seligman (2011) *Flourish*. Simon and Schuster

REFERENCES

1. The Changing Career Scene

1. John Davidson (2020) The robots are coming: 2.7 million Aussie jobs to disappear. https://www.afr.com/technology/the-robots-are-coming-2-7-million-aussie-jobs-to-disappear-20200310-p548nk
2. Raggatt, M. (2016) *Lawyers, doctors and public servants in firing line from rise of the machines*. Canberra Times 30 January 2016

    http://www.canberratimes.com.au/act-news/lawyers-doctors-and-public-servants-in-firing-line-from-rise-of-the-machines-20160127-gmf9kt.html

3. Work/life Balance

1. Stephen Covey (1989) The Seven Habits of Highly Effective People. The Business Library

6. Develop Talents and Strengths

1. {$NOTE_LABEL}. https://www.gallupstrengthscenter.com

7. Where Are You Now?

1. Price-Waterhouse Cooper, (2016) Putting Purpose to Work, a study of purpose in the workplace.

    https://www.pwc.com/us/en/about-us/corporate-responsibility/assets/pwc-putting-purpose-to-work-purpose-survey-report.pdf
2. NSW PUBLIC SERVICE COMMISSION | NSW PUBLIC SECTOR CAPABILITY FRAMEWORK VERSION 2: 2020

    https://www.psc.nsw.gov.au/sites/default/files/2020-11/capability_framework_v2_2020.pdf
3. https://www.psc.nsw.gov.au/sites/default/files/2020-11/capability_framework_v2_2020.pdf
4. https://www.psc.nsw.gov.au/sites/default/files/2020-11/capability_framework_v2_2020.pdf

8. Where Do You Want to Be

1. Amanda Reaume (2014) This CEO Quit a 100 Million Dollar Job to Spend More Time With His Daughter. Huffington Post
   https://www.huffingtonpost.ca/amanda-reaume/work-life-balance-dads_b_5903342.html

10. How's it Going Now?

1. Mini Habits by Stephen Guise, Core Message
   https://www.youtube.com/watch?v=rETOlen9G30
2. Stephen Covey (1990) Seven Habits of Highly Effective People. The Business Library

ABOUT THE AUTHOR

ANN ROLFE

Founder, Mentoring Works

Ann Rolfe has over 30 years' experience in adult learning, career coaching and mentoring. She is a certified Gallup Strengths Coach and Australia's most published author on mentoring.

Ann Rolfe has spoken international conferences in Australia, Canada, China, The Philippines, Singapore and USA. She has run workshops for people in fields as diverse as health, construction, energy, communications, education, law, and government.

She has developed award-winning mentoring programs for Aboriginal people and facilitated programs for women, graduates and injured people mentored by paralympians.

She runs regular webinars that are attended by participants all over the world and is the author of *Mentor Master Classes*, *Take a Minute to Mentor* and *Mentoring Mindset, Skills and Tools* currently in its fourth edition.

Contact: ann@mentoring-works.com

Or visit the website: www.mentoring-works.com

f